When FOOTBALL *Was* FOOTBALL

CHELSEA

CW00551613

© Haynes Publishing, 2015

The right of Andy Sherwood to be identified as the author of this Work has been asserted
by him in accordance with the Copyright, Designs & Patents Act 1988.

All rights reserved. No part of this publication may be reproduced, stored in a retrieval system
or transmitted, in any form or by any means, electronic, mechanical, photocopying, recording
or otherwise, without prior permission in writing from the publisher.

First published in 2010

A catalogue record for this book is available from the British Library

ISBN: 978-1-78521-026-6

Published by Haynes Publishing, Sparkford, Yeovil,
Somerset BA22 7JJ, UK
Tel: 01963 442030 Fax: 01963 440001
Int. tel: +44 1963 442030 Int. fax: +44 1963 440001
E-mail: sales@haynes.co.uk
Website: www.haynes.co.uk

Haynes North America Inc., 861 Lawrence Drive,
Newbury Park, California 91320, USA

All images © Mirrorpix

Creative Director: Kevin Gardner
Packaged for Haynes by BrainWave

Printed and bound in the US

When FOOTBALL *Was* FOOTBALL

CHELSEA

A Nostalgic Look at a Century of the Club

Andy Sherwood

Introduction

What defines a football club? Is it the bricks and mortar that bind the stadium? Is it £100,000 a week salaries, trophies, WAGS and Sky Sports subscriptions?

We'd argue that while football is all of these things now (some of them we like more than others), football's identity and heritage lies in its past, and that's no more evident than in the history of Chelsea.

You won't find yellow Nike footballs in this book. Or Lamborghinis. This is a history of Chelsea celebrating a more innocent time. A time when there was little difference between the lads who played for The Blues and the lads who watched them from The Shed. A time when the players and fans would often walk to the ground together, sometimes even drink together, and then part at the gates to take their respective places on the terraces and pitch.

Not all of these times are remembered through rose-tinted spectacles. Some periods have warts on them, including the decline of the 1970s and the rise of football hooliganism.

But what is quite obvious over these 200-odd pages is just how varied and rich is the history of the team from The Bridge is .

Contents

From a dormant first 50 years, trophy wise, to a first league title in 1955 and the heady days of the 1960s and early 1970s, The Blues were one of the most fashionable clubs in the country, adored by its public and celebrities alike.

The similarities between footballers "back in the day" and now are also poignant – they loved the same hobbies, such as golf, and even gave the same excuses for leaving clubs, such as wanting to return up north only to land at a London rival.

These photos were taken at a time when the top players in England would get a train home after winning an FA Cup Final. A time when phrases such as Image Rights didn't exist, and players would happily get snapped getting a haircut from their gaffer after winning a trophy, or show off their family caravan. Can you imagine Frank Lampard showing us his mobile home?

We know football is different now. It's more serious. It's a game where defeat can literally cost a team millions. Chelsea's fantastic side means you probably don't long for a return to the less successful days on the pitch, but this book will make you long for a return to a time *When Football Was Football*.

Andy Sherwood

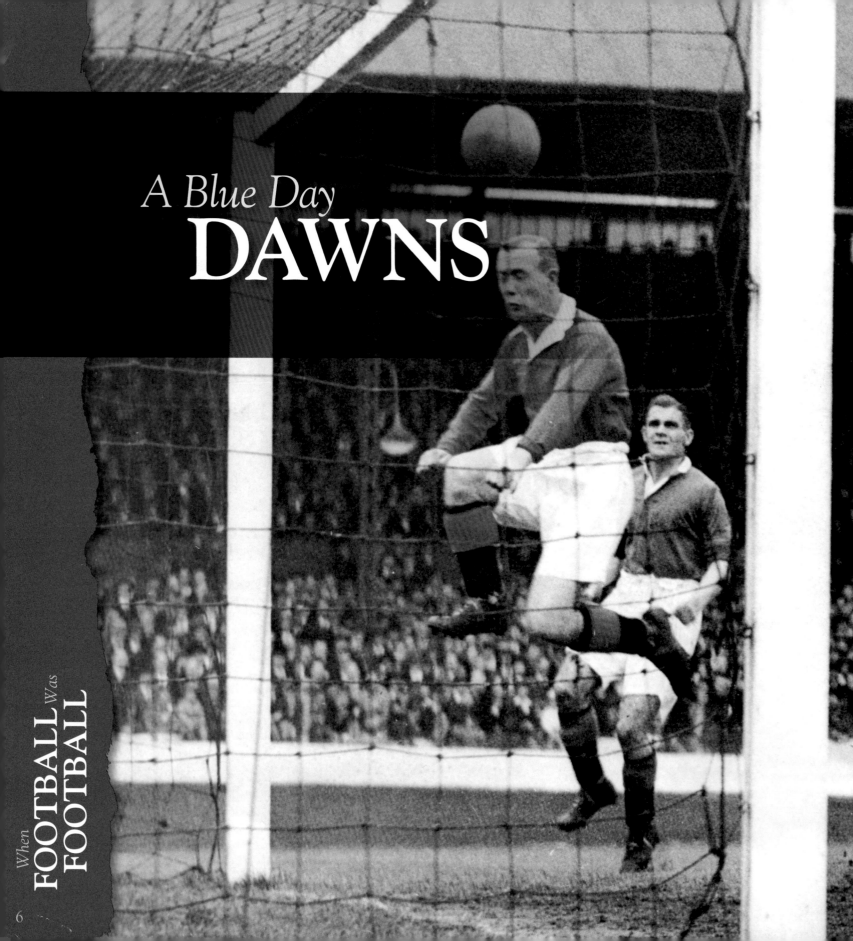

A Blue Day
DAWNS

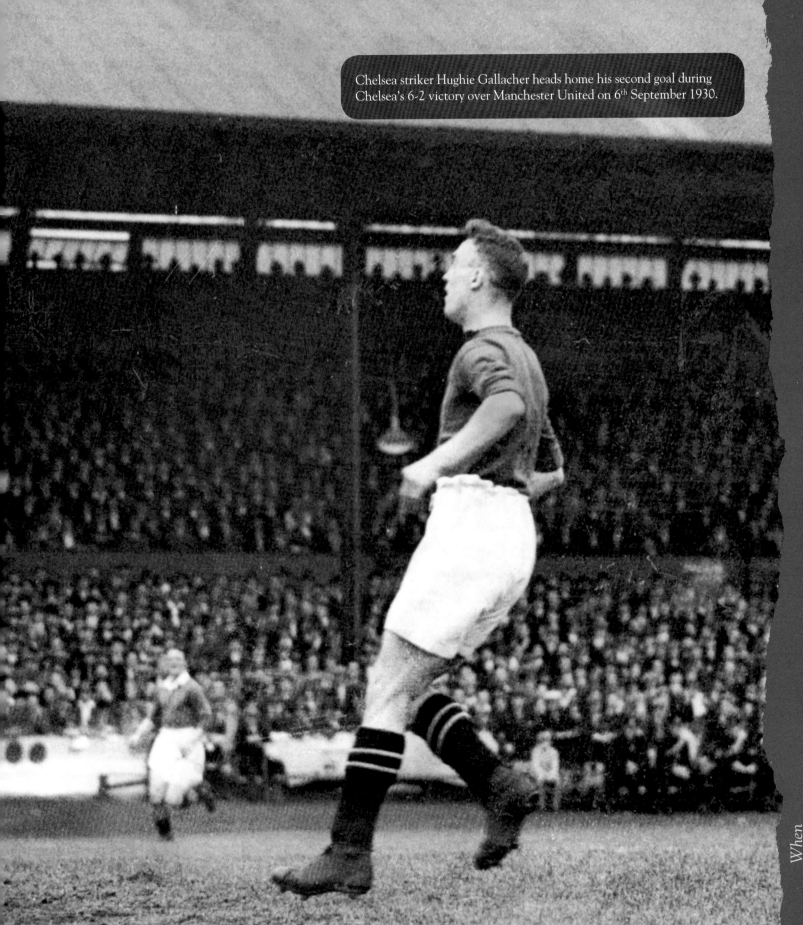

Chelsea striker Hughie Gallacher heads home his second goal during Chelsea's 6-2 victory over Manchester United on 6ᵗʰ September 1930.

1905 Chelsea FC formed at the Rising Sun pub on 14th March by brothers Henry (known as Gus) and Joseph Mears. Scottish international John Tait Robertson appointed the club's first player-manager. Chelsea play their first league match on 2nd September, losing 1-0 away at Stockport. **1907** Tommy Miller is Chelsea's first ever-present player in a season. **1907** David Calderhead is appointed manager, a role he holds for 26 years. **1911** A then record-setting 77,952 attend a fourth round FA Cup tie against Swindon on 11th March. **1915** Chelsea lose FA Cup Final 3-0 to Sheffield United. Game is called the Khaki Cup because of the large number of uniformed soldiers who attend. **1919** Beat Fulham 3-0 in the London Victory Challenge Cup Final at Highbury on 26th April. **1920** Finish third in the league, the highest finish for a London club. **1924** Relegated from top flight. **1930** Promoted back to the top flight. The club spends £25,000 on three big-name players: Scots Hughie Gallacher, Alex Jackson and Alec Cheyne. **1935** A crowd of 82,905 watch Chelsea play Arsenal at Stamford Bridge on 12th October. It is still a Blues record and the second highest attendance ever at an English league match. **1939** Former Queens Park Rangers' boss Billy Birrell named Chelsea manager shortly before the outbreak of the Second World War. **1939** Three games into the season first-class football is abandoned in Britain for the duration of the conflict. Only two members of Chelsea's 1938/9 squad play for them again.

Chelsea's squad knuckle down to pre-season training in August 1907.

LONDON'S COMING FOOTBALL SEASON.

Chelsea, who will be the second London team to appear in the First League battle, are taking the morning walk, which forms part of their training, on the fine cinder track at Stamford Bridge, Chelsea.—(Park.)

THE FAME GAME: Chelsea players give out autographs before a league match with Newcastle in February 1921.

The Bridge Is Born

Originally a home for the London Athletics Club, Stamford Bridge opened in 1877 to great fanfare. It was the home of athletics until 1904 and also hosted the 1898 Shinty World Championships. Then, brothers Gus and Joseph Mears acquired the lease. They had a dream – to see top-flight football being played at The Bridge. They tried to sell the stadium to Fulham, who declined, before deciding to start their own team to take on West London's top side. The architect who turned this athletics track into an arena fit for football was Archibald Leach, who designed 20 stadiums in his lifetime, including Anfield and Celtic Park. Some of the terracing was built from material excavated from the building of the Piccadilly Line.

Stamford Bridge pictured in September 1905 during Chelsea's 1-0 victory over West Brom.

The Bridge was used for many years as a neutral venue for Cup Finals. Huddersfield Town took on Preston North End there in the FA Cup Final in April 1922. Huddersfield won 1-0.

TOPICAL BUDGET

11

The Mirror Covers Chelsea

ENORMOUS CROWD WATCH LONDON'S FOOTBALL DERI

WOOLWICH ARSENAL BEAT CHELSEA IN THE LAST MINUTE.

CHELSEA FOOTBALL TEAM PRACTISING FOR THE COMING SEASON

Although it seems difficult to realise, the football season is close upon us, and the various teams are preparing for the fray. The photograph was taken yesterday evening at Stamford Bridge, where the Chelsea team played a trial match.

Stories about a girl being blinded by lightning and thunderstorms ending a heat wave were important in August 1909, but not as important as Chelsea returning to pre-season training, or "preparing for the fray", as the paper called it. It was The Blues who got the photo caption at a time when the *Mirror* had to choose its images sparingly and wisely.

The word "enormous" was often used by the *Mirror* to describe the attendances at Stamford Bridge – an apt description since crowds often topped 80,000. And they saw Chelsea dispatch Spurs 2-1 just before Christmas 1909 in what was "an exciting and interesting game".

TOTTENHAM LOSE TO CHELSEA AT STAMFORD BRIDGE.

There was an intensely exciting game at Stamford Bridge on Saturday, when Woolwich Arsenal beat Chelsea by 2 goals to 1. The final point was scored within a minute from time. (1) A tumble in front of the Arsenal's goal. (2) Macdonald, the Arsenal's goalkeeper, fisting out. (3) Headwork in mid-field. Jumping up, with arms outstretched, is Rouse, Chelsea's inside right. An idea of the enormous crowd present may be gained from the first picture.

It's a sickener for the 1908 Chelsea side as they're beaten 2-1 thanks to a last-minute Arsenal goal at Stamford Bridge in November. Chelsea's Fred Rouse, a striker who scored 11 goals in his one season at The Bridge, can be seen in the bottom right picture with his arms out.

There was an enormous crowd at Stamford Bridge on Saturday, when Chelsea beat Tottenham Hotspur by two goals to one, after an exciting and interesting game. The picture was taken during an attack on the Chelsea goal.

William "Fatty" Foulke

It was obvious who'd eaten all the pies in 1905. It was Chelsea's first ever goalkeeper, William Foulke, pictured above making a great save during a match against Bradford City at Stamford Bridge in January 1906. He got his unfortunate nickname because he was a big lad, weighing in at 22 stone. Foulke was tall as well, at 6ft 4in, a useful frame to have when defending corners. He was also a professional cricketer, and joined Chelsea from Sheffield United for £50 with something of a reputation. In 1902 he chased a referee while naked after a disputed goal in the FA Cup Final against Southampton. The referee had to hide in a broom cupboard. His erratic behaviour continued at The Bridge. If he thought his defence wasn't trying hard enough, he would walk off the pitch. Foulke is credited with the creation of ball boys, as Chelsea would place two lads behind the goal to draw attention to William's size. The kids eventually started throwing balls back. Fatty only played for Chelsea for one season, making 35 appearances.

A Stage For All Occasions

Baseball matches were played at The Bridge twice before the 1930s. In 1918, a crowd of 38,000 watched an exhibition match between the US Army and the Canadians, and in October 1924 the Chicago White Sox and New York Giants played a series of matches in Britain and Ireland, including one at Stamford Bridge, pictured above.

The Daily Mirror

THE MORNING JOURNAL WITH THE SECOND LARGEST NET SALE

No. 2,550. Registered at the G.P.O. as a Newspaper. WEDNESDAY, DECEMBER 27, 1911. One Halfpenny.

A WET AND DISMAL BOXING DAY IN LONDON: SPECTATORS WATCH FOOTBALL MATCHES FROM UNDER UMBRELLAS.

n direct contrast to Christmas Day. On Monday the
 pleasant, but yesterday they were as dismal as they
steadily nearly all day, and so persistent was the down-
 m of the footballer was damped, the crowds at the big

London matches being much smaller than on the previous day. (1) A section of the
crowd at the Fulham v. Chelsea match at Stamford Bridge. Note the umbrellas.
(2) Watching the Woolwich Arsenal v. Tottenham Hotspur match at Plumstead.
There are many vacant spaces. —[*Daily Mirror* photographs.]

Rehearsal for the Football Season.

LARGE CROWD WATCHES CHELSEA'S PRACTICE GAME.

Though the curtain will not be rung up on the football season until August has finished its run,
thousands of spectators attended dress-rehearsals of the large London clubs on Saturday. The picture
shows Chelsea's second team goalkeeper effecting a smart save.—[*Daily Mirror* photograph.]

It's Boxing Day in December 1911 and London is a washout.
While the crowds didn't show at Plumstead for Arsenal vs
Spurs in the bottom picture, the terraces at Stamford Bridge
were heaving for Chelsea vs Fulham.

Thousands of supporters flocked to The Bridge to see pre-
season training in 1908.

15

The crowd watch Chelsea take on Spurs in the FA Cup in February 1910. Chelsea lost what the *Mirror* called a "splendid game".

Play And They Will Come

The Bridge is swarmed in December 1909 for Chelsea's game with Newcastle. Many people got in without paying, making recording the attendance a logistical nightmare. One number that Chelsea fans did remember from the day was the score – a 2-1 win.

Another record-breaking crowd in March 1911, when 77,952 attended a fourth round FA Cup tie against Swindon, which Chelsea won 3-1.

The Gentlemen's Game

Chelsea skipper Andy Wilson, who made 253 appearances for the club between 1923 and 1931, and his Arsenal counterpart Tom Parker, shake hands before their London derby in January 1930.

Jack Cock

Cock was a prolific star for The Pensioners, scoring 53 goals in 110 appearances between 1919 and 1923. Signed from a cash-strapped Huddersfield for £2,500, he scored twice on his debut and notched 24 in his first season. He'd go on to manage Millwall against Chelsea in 1945. He had a booming tenor voice and starred in music hall productions before turning to a career many footballers have found solace in – running a pub.

Golf has been the traditional vice of footballers since the game was invented, and they loved it just as much in the 1920s as they do now. Pictured below is Jack Cock (left), playing a tournament against the Co-Op.

A Golden Era

The 1929 squad at Waterloo Station, heading off for a tour of South Africa in May.
The team won promotion back to the top flight at the end of the following season.

Chelsea stars John Priestley, Sidney Castle and Harold Miller find a novel way to get
ready for the new season in August 1924. The three of them played 599 times for the club.

Chelsea defeating Everton 2-0 in the FA Cup in January 1929.

-LEGENDS-

Hughie Gallacher

Long before the likes of Gazza, football had another troubled genius from a working-class background. Gallacher was born in Bellshill, Scotland, and worked 10-hour shifts in the Hattonrigg Pit at the age of 15, before joining Queen Of The South in 1920. After spells with Airdrieonians and Newcastle, the striker joined Chelsea in 1930 for £10,000 and was one of the greatest players of his generation. He was small for a footballer, standing just 5ft 5in high, but what he lacked in stature he made up for with ability. He was the all-round player, able to pass with either foot, dribble, and get stuck in with some feisty tackles, and he scored 23 goals in 20 games for Scotland. During his stint at Chelsea, he was banned for two months for swearing at a referee and was declared bankrupt in 1934 due to a long-winded and fraught divorce. Hughie tragically committed suicide in 1957.

Hughie (right) with Blues winger Alex Jackson in February 1931.

Gallacher in action for The Blues during a Division One match in December 1930.

FOOTBALL
–STATS–

Hughie Gallacher

Name: Hugh Kilpatrick Gallacher

Born: Bellshill, Scotland 1903

Died: 1957

Position: Centre-forward

League Career: 1921–1939

Chelsea Career: 1930–1934

Club Appearances: 144

Goals: 81

Scotland Appearances: 20

Goals: 23

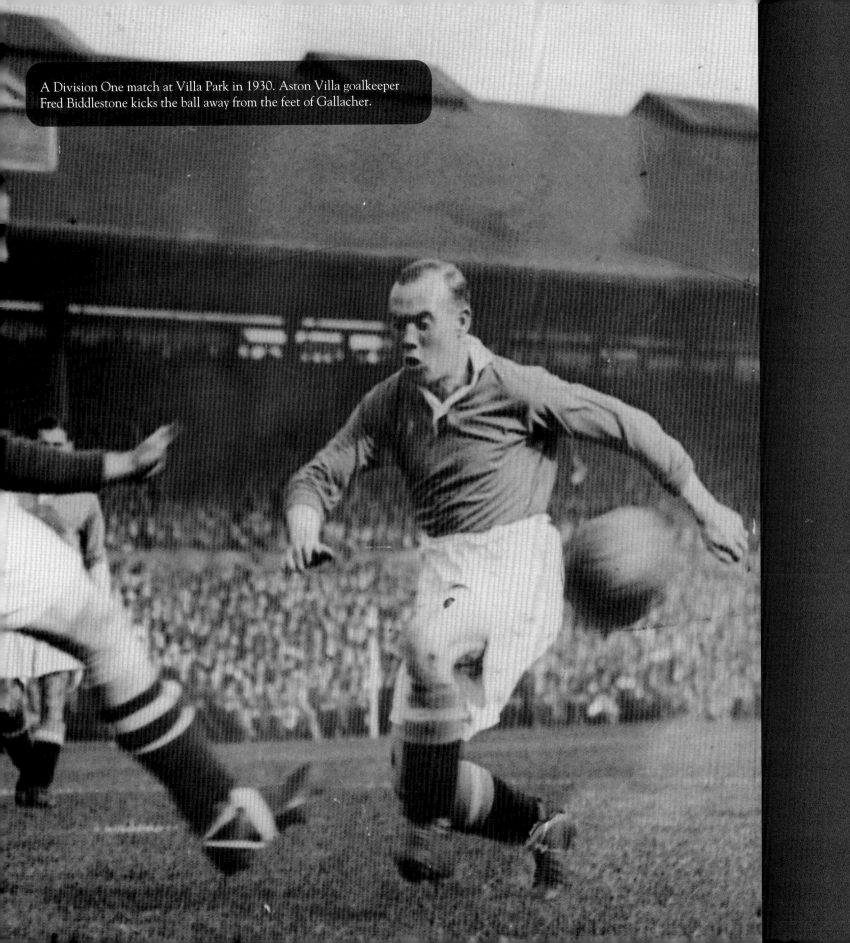

A Division One match at Villa Park in 1930. Aston Villa goalkeeper Fred Biddlestone kicks the ball away from the feet of Gallacher.

Three of Chelsea's top strikers in February 1931. Clearly the days before the public knew smoking wouldn't improve an athlete's performance. Left to right: Andy Wilson, Hughie Gallacher and Jackie Crawford.

The team trains during the 1930/1 season: Left to right: Alex Jackson, Tommy Law, Andy Wilson, Alec Cheyne, George Barber, Sam Irving and George Pearson.

Wartime
BLUES

Chelsea and Charlton fans mingle at The Valley during a match in December 1937, just before the outbreak of the Second World War.

1939 Chelsea field guest players during the Second World War, most notably Manchester United legend Matt Busby. **1944** Lose the Football War League Cup Final to Charlton on 15th April, 3-1. **1945** Return to the final a year later on 7th April and this time they beat Millwall 2-0. **1945** The war ends and the English football authorities play a series of matches to celebrate world peace. As part of a goodwill gesture, Chelsea take on Dynamo Moscow, reigning champions of the Soviet Union. The match takes place on 13th November at Stamford Bridge. **1946** Following the war, Chelsea again spend big, and again buy three big-name forwards: Tommy Lawton, Len Goulden and Tommy Walker sign for around £22,000. **1947** Lawton sets a new club record by scoring 26 goals in 34 league games. **1948** Striker Roy Bentley joins from Newcastle United for £11,500.

Billy Birrell

The first 50 years of Chelsea's history were somewhat uneventful when it came to winning trophies. But one man from that era is responsible for implementing a system that helped transform The Blues into one of the most dominant forces in football. Billy Birrell, pictured below right, in 1938, was in charge from 1939 until 1952. He didn't win many trophies, and the club were nearly relegated under him in 1951, but his best work took place off the pitch. Frustrated by rising transfer costs, he focused on setting up an academy that eventually discovered players such as Jimmy Greaves and Ron Harris. His planning paved the way for Ted Drake to win the league in 1955.

Joe Payne

Signed just as the Second World War started, Joe Payne scored 23 goals in 47 appearances. Whilst on Chelsea's books until 1946, the almost complete cancellation of matches during this period meant Chelsea never saw the best from this canny striker. He still holds a record to this day for scoring 10 goals in a 12-0 win for Luton over Bristol Rovers in April 1936.

It's a sell-out against Dynamo Moscow in 1945 – and the doors are locked. Almost 100,000 people saw the match.

31

From Russia With Love

Chelsea line up before their post-war match with Dynamo Moscow. Chelsea wore an unfamiliar red stripe due to a clash with Dynamo's blue kit. Before kick-off, the Dynamo players presented a bouquet of flowers to their opposite numbers. The final score was 3-3, with Moscow impressing the crowd by fighting back to secure a draw after being 2-0 and 3-2 down.

Fans clamour for a view of the Moscow game, which indicates that many more than the recorded 100,000 probably saw the match.

This is Chelsea's war-time equivalent to Ian Hutchinson, long-throw expert Sam Weaver. Photographed here in 1932 while playing for Newcastle, he joined Chelsea in 1936 for just over £4,100 and played for them during the Second World War, making 125 appearances, before leaving in 1946 for Stockport County.

The left-half was also skipper for The Blues and was a guest player for Leeds in 1942/3. He was part of a Chelsea side that didn't win many trophies but was often regarded a joy to watch. Like Hutchinson, Weaver came from Derbyshire and just like Hutchinson, discovered his talent in training by accident.

ABOVE: Continuing the tradition of hitting a slightly smaller ball, Chelsea's Roy Bentley and Denis Compton (far right) play a spot of golf before the 1950 FA Cup semi-final.

RIGHT: Roy and Ken Armstrong head off for the next hole.

The Big Spenders

After the Second World War, Chelsea became one of the big players in the transfer market. The ambitious board, frustrated at the lack of trophies at The Bridge, signed three forwards – Tommy Lawton, Len Goulden and Tommy Walker – for around £22,000. Lawton set a new club record by scoring 26 goals in 34 league games in 1946/7 but was sold to Notts County after falling out with Billy Birrell. His replacement was Roy Bentley, signed from Newcastle United for £11,500 in 1948. Pictured right is the 1948 Board Of Directors. Sitting on the far left is Billy Birrell. Chairman Joe Mears sits third from the right.

RIGHT: Chelsea's squad in 1949. Left to right, standing: Billy Birrell, Reg Williams, Roy Bentley, Frank Mitchell, Harry Medhurst, Billy Hughes, Stan Willemse, N Smith (trainer). Seated: Bobby Campbell, Hugh Billington, Thomas Jenkins, John Harris, Len Goulden, Danny Winter, Ken Armstrong. On the ground: Jimmy Bowie (left) and Billy Gray.

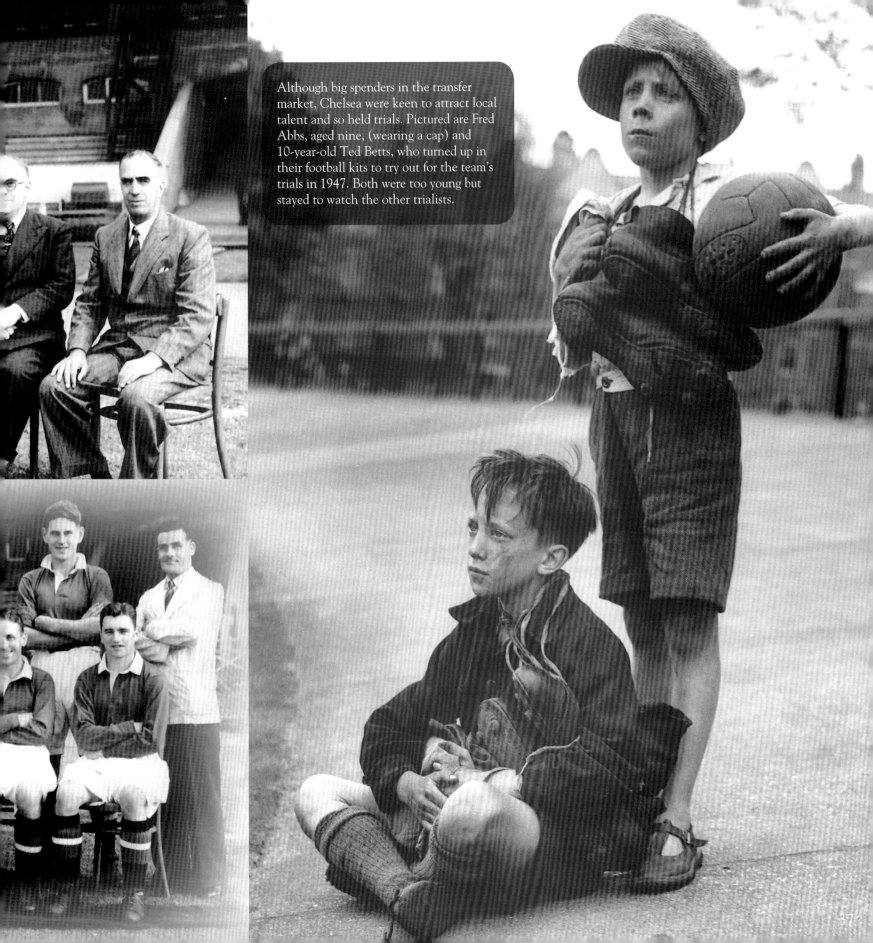

Although big spenders in the transfer market, Chelsea were keen to attract local talent and so held trials. Pictured are Fred Abbs, aged nine, (wearing a cap) and 10-year-old Ted Betts, who turned up in their football kits to try out for the team's trials in 1947. Both were too young but stayed to watch the other trialists.

–LEGENDS–

Harry Medhurst

Popular keeper Harry started out at Woking before joining West Ham in 1938. He moved to Chelsea in 1946 in exchange for Joe Payne, who went the other way. Renowned for his spectacular saves at full-stretch, Harry played for Chelsea for six years and would return to the club as first team trainer in the 1960s and 1970s. A keen gardener, he kept 32 clean sheets and is one of Chelsea's top 10 goalkeepers of all time.

FOOTBALL –STATS–

Harry Medhurst

Name: Harry Medhurst

Born: Woking, 1916

Died: 1984

Position: Goalkeeper

Playing Career: 1938–1952

Chelsea Career: 1946–1952

Club Appearances: 157

Goals: 0

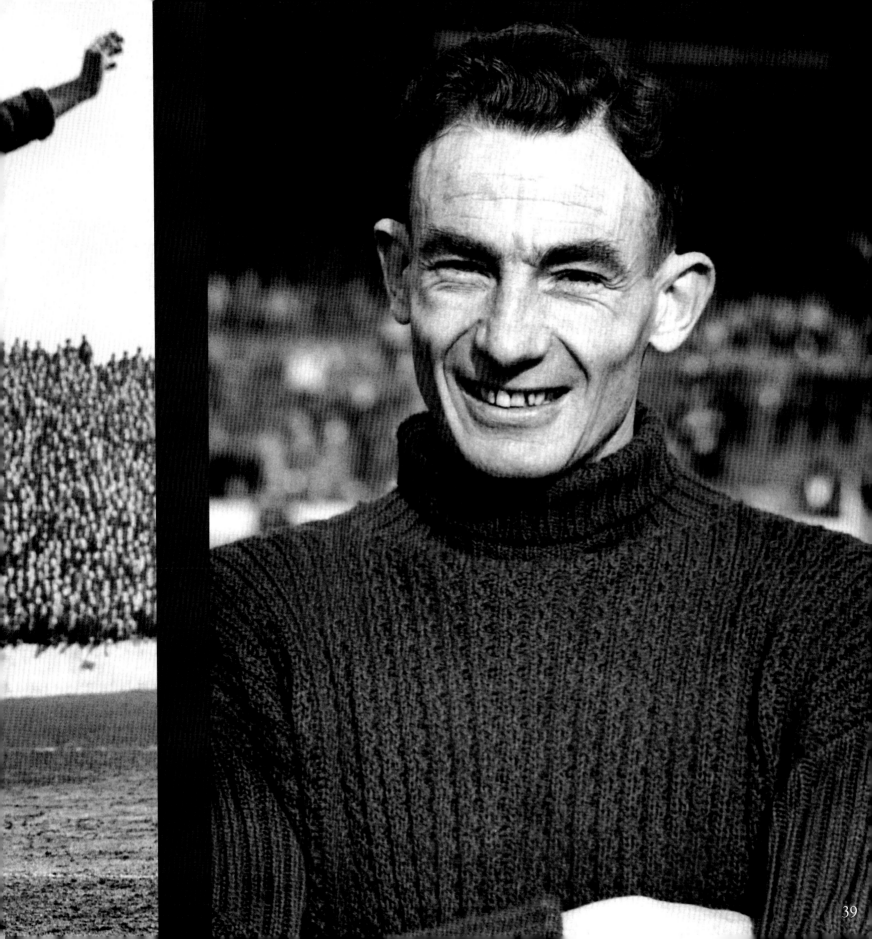

Medhurst makes himself big during Chelsea's 2-0 win over Manchester United in the FA Cup in March 1950.

So close but so far: Chelsea got to the semi-final of the 1950 FA Cup, losing a replay 1-0 to Arsenal after the first match ended 2-2.

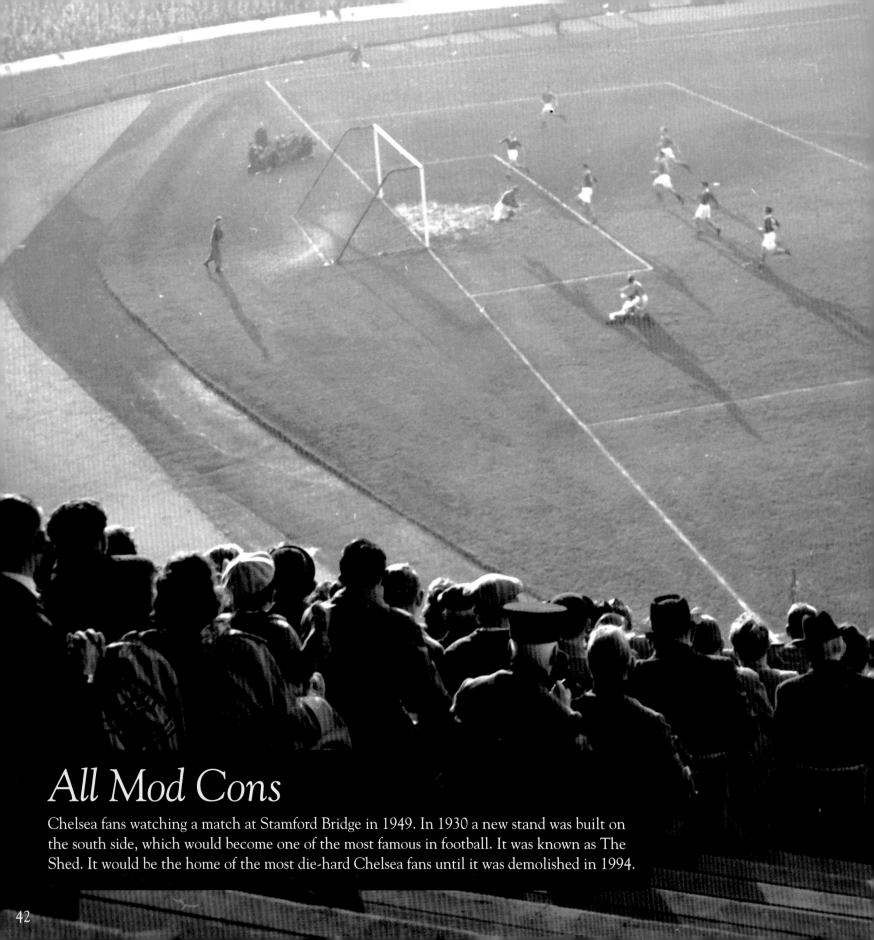

All Mod Cons

Chelsea fans watching a match at Stamford Bridge in 1949. In 1930 a new stand was built on the south side, which would become one of the most famous in football. It was known as The Shed. It would be the home of the most die-hard Chelsea fans until it was demolished in 1994.

Tommy Walker

When the football calendar was abandoned at the outbreak of the Second World War, Chelsea were reduced to playing regional competitions such as the games against Charlton and Millwall in the Football League War Cup. With most of the squad overseas fighting in the war, guest players donned the blue shirt. One player to guest for Chelsea in 1944 and 1945 was Hearts star Tommy, a well-respected and much loved Scottish international who was called "Football's First Gentleman". His career in football was in the balance when he nearly became a minister for the Church of Scotland. He joined the army in 1938 as a sergeant in the Signals Regiment, went to India, but still managed to play the game, including turning out for the Army's "All Stars" Team. Chelsea were so impressed by his wartime appearances they paid Hearts £6,000 for his services to play alongside Tommy Lawton. He returned to Hearts in 1948 as assistant manager.

Magic feet—No. 3

Here is a farewell picture of Tommy Walker, Chelsea's inside left. At Portsmouth on Boxing Day he plays his last game in English football. Then Soccer's First Gentleman, capped fourteen times for Scotland, goes home to be assistant manager of Hearts, the club with which he began his brilliant career at the age of 17.

There has never been a more popular player than the Ace of Hearts. A First Division player once said: " The lowest thing in football is a foul against Tommy Walker."

A free-kick against him is a rare event. WHY IS HE A STAR? He is 5ft. 8in., 12st., of boundless, intelligent energy. Watch him as he moves shrewdly clear of the opposition. Note the compactness of ball and man when he sets off on those mazy, top-speed thrusts with the ball under perfect control. And see how he catches defences flat-footed with cross-field passes. He is as much at home at wing half as at inside right or left.

And for your album here are his autograph and a print of his left foot.

The *Mirror* pays tribute to Tommy's magic feet in his last appearance for Chelsea in 1948, against Portsmouth. The article describes his mazy runs and perfect ball control, claiming, "The lowest thing in football is a foul against Tommy."

43

REVOLUTIONS

Chelsea's A & B teams in pre-season training at Stamford Bridge in August 1952, which was Ted Drake's first season in charge as manager.

1951 Chelsea are six points from safety and facing relegation with four games to go. They win their next three matches and head into their final match needing to beat Bolton Wanderers while fellow relegation candidates Sheffield Wednesday beat Everton. Chelsea win 4-0, and Wednesday beat Everton 6-0, and survive. 1951 With rising transfer fees crippling many clubs, manager Billy Birrell develops a new youth and scouting programme. It provides the core of Chelsea's first team for the next three decades, producing such players as Jimmy Greaves, Peter Osgood, Peter Bonetti, Ray Wilkins, Ron Harris, Bobby Tambling, Alan Hudson, Terry Venables and John Hollins. 1952 Former Arsenal and England striker Ted Drake is appointed manager. Ted replaces The Pensioners emblem with a lion crest. 1955 Chelsea win the league in the club's Jubilee year. Their points total of 52 that season remains one of the lowest to have secured the English League title since the First World War. 1955 The Blues are crowned Charity Shield Winners, beating Newcastle United 3-0. Bentley and Blunstone are the scorers, the third was an own goal. 1957 Jimmy Greaves scores on his debut for Chelsea. 1958 Preston and Chelsea players lead a minute's silence at the start of their game in February in tribute to the victims of the Manchester United Munich air crash.

Stan Willemse in action against Manchester United at Old Trafford during a 2-0 defeat in August 1952.

Drake's Ducklings

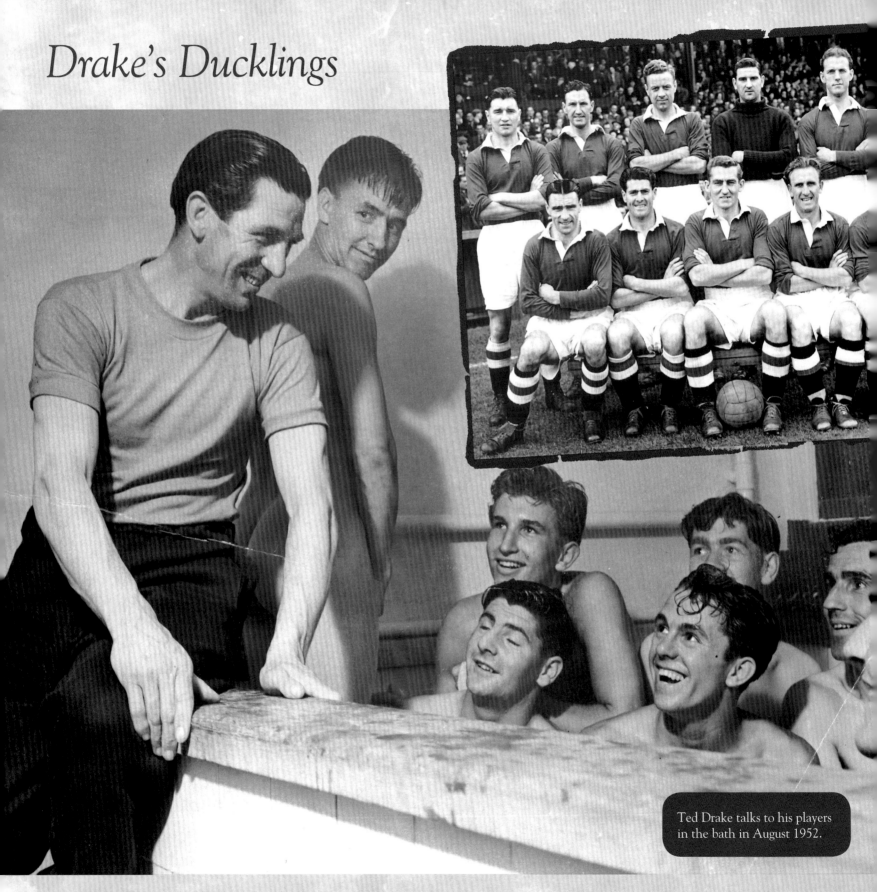

Ted Drake talks to his players in the bath in August 1952.

Ted Drake

Chelsea's 1952 side: Left to right, standing: Ken Armstrong, John Harris, John Saunders, Bill Robertson, Bill Dickson, Stan Willemse. Seated: Bobby Campbell, John McNichol, Roy Bentley, Eric Parsons and Billy Gray.

The gaffer Ted Drake making plans with Chelsea's Roy Bentley and staff in April 1955. The team won the league title that month.

FOOTBALL
—STATS—
Ted Drake

Name: Edward Joseph Drake

Born: Southampton, 1912

Died: Raynes Park, 1995

Position: Centre-forward

Playing Career: 1931–1945

Chelsea Manager: 1952–1961

England Appearances: 5

Goals: 6

Clubs Played For:
Southampton, Arsenal

Clubs Managed: Hendon, Reading, Chelsea

While former manager Billy Birrell is credited with starting the youth policy that made Chelsea one of the biggest names in football, it was Drake who revolutionized the club and set it on the road to glory. Ted was one of football's first tracksuit managers. He was loved by players and fans alike and won the league title in 1955. He would shake each player by the hand and wish them all the best before a match. One of his first actions was to remove the image of a Chelsea Pensioner from the match programme – the club's old nickname was no more. From then on they were to be known as The Blues and the emblem on the shirt was replaced with a lion. "I want more people to live, sleep, breathe Chelsea Football Club," he demanded of the club's normally polite, sporting crowd. He introduced ball work at training – a radical departure at the time.

Chelsea's John McNichol heads away during a League Division One match against Sheffield United in September 1953, which ended in a 2-1 defeat for The Blues. McNichol, a centre-forward, played 202 times for Chelsea, scoring 66 goals. He was Ted Drake's first signing for the club. A near ever-present in Chelsea's first title-winning side of 1955, notching 14 goals, he stayed at Chelsea for three more seasons but later lost his place in the side to Jimmy Greaves.

The View From The Top

Chelsea home games were often sell-outs, and people went to great lengths to watch their heroes in action. This shot is from Chelsea vs Arsenal in April 1953. Some fans who could not get a seat found their way to the roof of the grandstand and watched the game from this lofty vantage point.

The Kids Are Alright

The success of Billy Birrell's youth development scheme projected the club to new heights in the 1950s. Here, the youth team train in March 1953.

–LEGENDS– Roy Bentley

Roy Bentley joined Chelsea for medical reasons, following his doctor's advice in 1948 in a bid to cure a lung problem. The prolific striker signed for £12,500 as a replacement for Tommy Lawton, who bizarrely also joined The Blues looking for a cure to a similar medical condition. It took Chelsea fans time to warm to the powerful, deep-lying forward, who only scored three times in the first four months of his Blues career. But he went on to become a legend, scoring 22 goals in his first season, and earning an England cap, the first of 12. He was skipper when Chelsea won the league for the first time in 1955 and is third in the all-time goalscorers list at Chelsea, tied with Peter Osgood. He was top scorer in each of his eight seasons at the club. He left amid controversy in 1956 for West London rivals Fulham, who converted him to a centre-half. Bentley's era was different from the modern game in so many ways. "Few players had cars," he once said. "It was one of my ambitions to buy a car and drive to my parents' street in Bristol."

Bentley turns down Bristol City for Fulham in 1956.

Roy Bentley leads his team out for a match against Sheffield Wednesday in April 1955. Chelsea won 3-0 and were crowned champions.

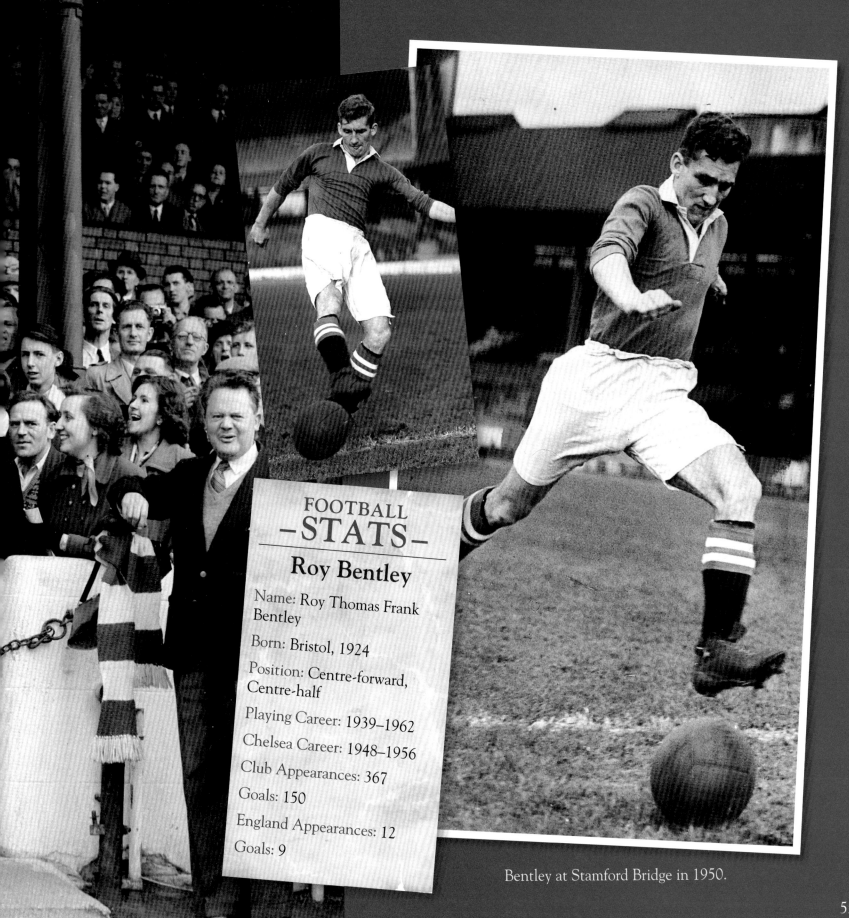

FOOTBALL
–STATS–

Roy Bentley

Name: Roy Thomas Frank Bentley

Born: Bristol, 1924

Position: Centre-forward, Centre-half

Playing Career: 1939–1962

Chelsea Career: 1948–1956

Club Appearances: 367

Goals: 150

England Appearances: 12

Goals: 9

Bentley at Stamford Bridge in 1950.

Billy Gray gives boxing lessons at Salesian College, Hammersmith in April 1953. The skilful winger made 172 appearances for Chelsea from 1949 to 1953, scoring 15 goals.

A Man's Game

Ground staff at White Hart Lane clearing the pitch for the FA Cup semi-final between Arsenal and Chelsea in April 1952.

Long before the days of undersoil heating and players wearing gloves, football was often played in harsh conditions. Above, Chelsea players train in the snow in 1955. But even this was mild in comparison to what footballers had experienced before: in October 1932, it was so cold at Chelsea's match with Blackpool that five Chelsea players left the pitch before the end of the game. Blackpool won 4-0.

Chelsea supporters watch their team from the stands at Stamford Bridge in August 1954, little knowing they were watching a championship-winning side.

Chelsea defeating Burnley 1-0 in a League Division
One match at Stamford Bridge in August 1954.

Chelsea play West Brom during the 1954/5 season. The Blues are attacking the Albion goal at Stamford Bridge during a game that finished 3-3.

Champions

Chelsea's team in 1954 clicked like never before, thanks to a great mixture of grit and flair in the squad assembled by Drake. The stars included keeper Charlie "Chick" Thomson, amateur players Derek Saunders and Jim Lewis, central midfielder Johnny "Jock" McNichol, wingers Eric "Rabbit" Parsons and Frank Blunstone, defender Peter Sillett and future England manager Ron Greenwood in central defence. Club stalwarts right-back Ken Armstrong, left-back Stan Willemse and veteran defender John Harris completed the line-up. Perhaps the only genuine star in the side was captain, top scorer (with 21 league goals) and England international Bentley. As well as winning the league, they won the Charity Shield the following season.

Chelsea's 1954/5 team photo. Left to right, standing: Stan Willemse, Ken Armstrong, Peter Sillett, Stan Wicks, Chick Thomson, Derek Saunders, John Harris. Seated: Eric Parsons, John McNichol, Roy Bentley, Ted Drake (manager), Seamus O'Connell, Frank Blunstone. Inserts: Bill Robertson (left) and Les Stubbs.

Action during Chelsea's last home game against Sheffield Wednesday, which they won 3-0 and were crowned champions in April 1955.

The Party Starts

Roy Bentley and the Chelsea players in the stands
celebrating their league victory.

The final whistle goes and Chelsea are champions. Fans and photographers gather on the pitch as The Blues confirm the league title by defeating Sheffield Wednesday 3-0 on 23rd April 1955.

Loyal Supporters

Ted Drake shaking hands with an apparently unimpressed supporter before Chelsea's game with Wednesday in 1955. He was in fact the 1,000,000th spectator to walk through the turnstiles during the 1954/5 season.

Blunstone (pictured right), the Chelsea outside-left, dribbles the ball past Rudman, the Burnley full-back. It led to a Chelsea goal in a 2-0 FA Cup victory in February 1956. Jimmy Greaves once claimed that Blunstone had a heart the size of a cabbage. He starred for Chelsea for nine years, scoring 54 goals in 347 appearances. He played on after a broken leg robbed him of some of his pace, but couldn't help suffering the same injury again, and retired in 1964.

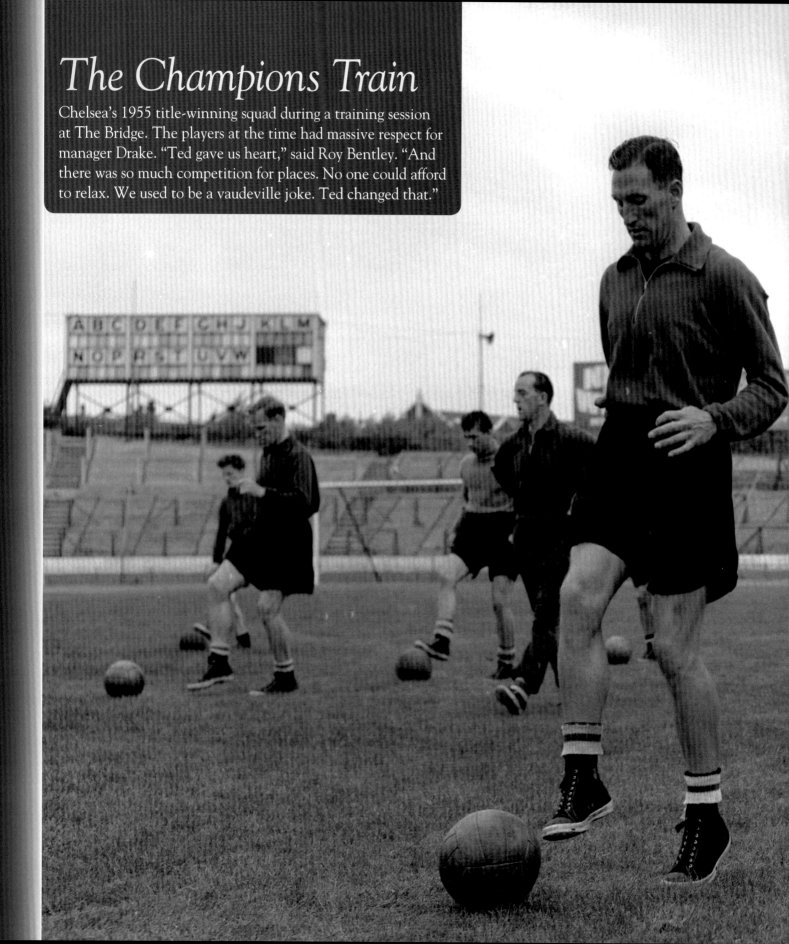

The Champions Train

Chelsea's 1955 title-winning squad during a training session at The Bridge. The players at the time had massive respect for manager Drake. "Ted gave us heart," said Roy Bentley. "And there was so much competition for places. No one could afford to relax. We used to be a vaudeville joke. Ted changed that."

Preston and Chelsea players lead a minute's silence at the start of their game in tribute to the victims of the Manchester United Munich air crash in February 1958.

–LEGENDS–

Jimmy Greaves

One of the greatest strikers ever to play the game was a product of the Chelsea youth team. Greaves was a sensational talent. He scored on his debut in 1957 against Spurs (a feat he managed for all the clubs he played for), and he finished as top scorer four seasons in a row between 1957 and 1961. In 1960 he became the youngest ever player to score 100 league goals in English football at the age of 21 (and at the age of 23 matched Dixie Dean's record of 200 goals).

His tally of 41 league goals in the 1960/1 season remains a club record. Unbelievably, Chelsea didn't win a major honour during Jimmy's time at the club. He broke West London hearts in 1961, moving to AC Milan. Yet despite scoring nine goals in 12 matches, he failed to settle there and returned to sign for London rivals Spurs, ironically the team he scored against on his Chelsea debut.

> *I was just a kid playing it off the cuff without fear.*
>
> Jimmy Greaves

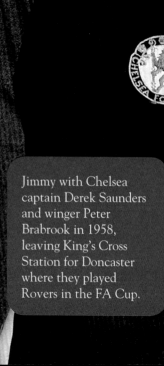

Jimmy with Chelsea captain Derek Saunders and winger Peter Brabrook in 1958, leaving King's Cross Station for Doncaster where they played Rovers in the FA Cup.

FOOTBALL
–STATS–
Jimmy Greaves

Name: James Peter Greaves

Born: East Ham, 1940

Position: Striker

Playing Career: 1957–1979

Chelsea Career: 1957–1961

Club Appearances: 169

Goals: 132

England Appearances: 57

Goals: 44

Jimmy Greaves playing cricket for the Chelsea Cricket XI in August 1958.

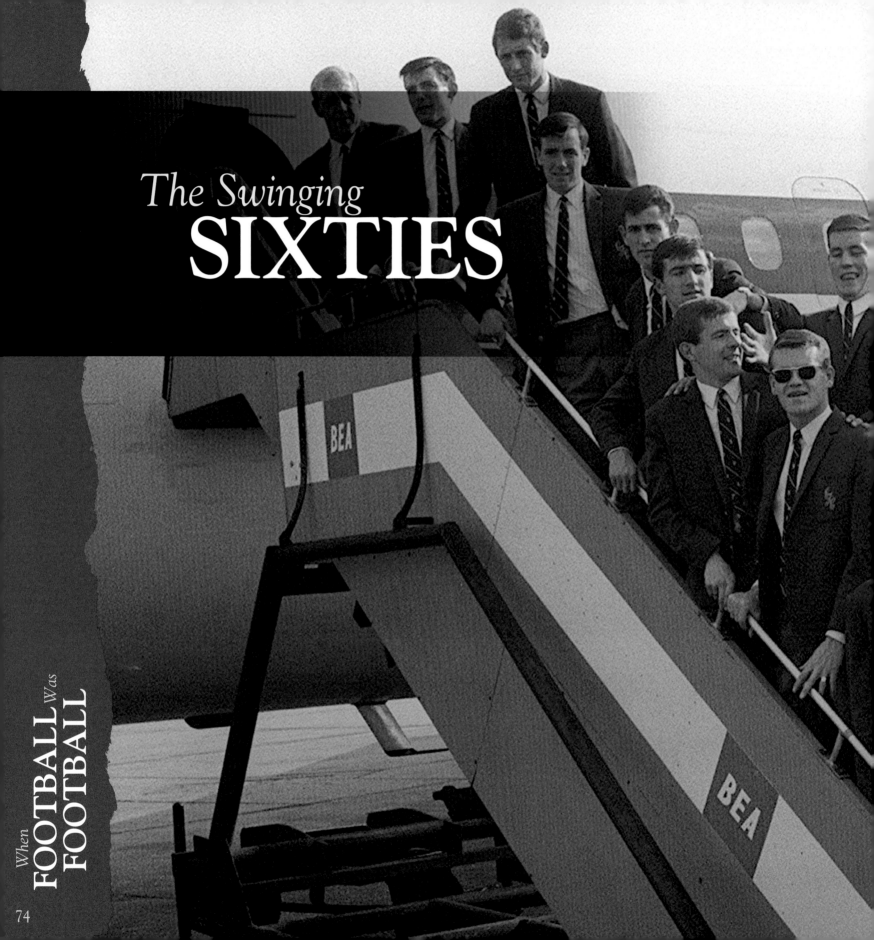

The Swinging
SIXTIES

The Chelsea squad head to Düsseldorf and the Fairs Cup in 1965 for their match with TSV 1860 München.

1961 Jimmy Greaves scores four goals in his final match for the club against Nottingham Forest on 29th April. **1961** Tommy Docherty appointed manager. **1962** Relegated: Docherty starts to rebuild the squad. Ron "Chopper" Harris makes his debut. **1963** Promoted as Second Division runners-up, secured with a crucial 1-0 win against rivals Sunderland and a 7-0 final day win over Portsmouth. **1964** Finish fifth in first season back in top flight. **1965** Docherty sends home eight key players (Venables, Graham, Bridges, Hollins, McCreadie, Hinton, Murray and Joe Fascione) for breaking a curfew before a crucial match against Burnley. A team of reserves and youngsters are beaten 6-2 as the title challenge collapses; Chelsea eventually finished third. **1965** Lose FA Cup semi-final to Liverpool 2-0 but win the League Cup, beating Leicester City. **1966** Lose in semi-final of Fairs Cup to Barcelona. **1966** Docherty sells Venables, Graham, Bridges and Murray during the summer. Scottish winger Charlie Cooke joins for £72,000, as does striker Tommy Baldwin, who arrives in part-exchange for Graham. **1967** Lose to Tottenham Hotspur in the first all-London FA Cup Final, known as the Cockney Cup Final. **1967** Peter Bonetti wins first ever Chelsea Player Of The Year Award. **1967** Docherty departs, Dave Sexton takes charge.

Chelsea's 1960 line-up: Left to right, standing: Peter Brabrook, Bobby Evans, Peter Sillett, Peter Bonetti, Charley Livesey, John Sillett, Terry Bradbury. Seated: Johnny Brooks, Terry Venables, Jimmy Greaves and Frank Blunstone.

Forest goalkeeper Peter Grummitt grabs hold of the ball as Greaves gets ready to pounce during The Blues' 4-3 win at The Bridge.

Farewell Jimmy

One of the saddest days in the history of Chelsea has to be Jimmy Greaves' last match for the club against Nottingham Forest before signing for AC Milan. He scored four goals that day, a fitting end to his career in West London. He never really wanted to move to Italy and practically begged the club not to let him go. After 12 games he signed for Spurs for £99,999. He wanted to return to Stamford Bridge but the club refused to beat their North London rivals' offer, leaving Jimmy hurt and with a cockerel on his shirt instead of a lion. Jimmy was part of a golden era for football, where there was little difference between the players and fans. "When I first joined Chelsea we caught the underground to Fulham Broadway then walked to the ground with the supporters," he once said. "We chatted freely until we got to The Bridge when we went through the players' entrance and they went through the turnstiles; that was the only difference between us. Now if players don't drive themselves, they arrive in heavily guarded coaches."

—LEGENDS—

Tommy Docherty

There aren't many managers in the history of the game like Tommy. After joining as player-coach under Ted Drake in 1961 (he was brought in by the Board – a decision which didn't make Drake happy at all), he took over the reins less than 12 months later. The side was still reeling from the loss of Greaves, and he joined too late to prevent relegation, but Docherty immediately set about restoring the team's pride and status in football. He changed the kit to blue shorts and white socks and imposed a regime of strict discipline. He sold off many of the club's older players and replaced them with the talented youngsters emerging from the youth squad.

He also had a canny knack of finding bargains in the transfer market. The result? Promotion the following season as Second Division runners-up, secured with a crucial and hard-fought 1-0 win at rivals Sunderland (and a now legendary goal scored by Tommy Harmer's groin) and a 7-0 final day win over Portsmouth. Thanks to Docherty, Chelsea returned to the top of football with a team full of youth and spirit, including Harris and Bonetti, winger Bobby Tambling (whose 202 goals in 370 games remain a club record), midfielder John Hollins, full-back Ken Shellito, striker Barry Bridges, winger Bert Murray and captain and playmaker Terry Venables. His team became known as the Diamonds, after he called them "little diamonds" on a TV documentary. Striker George Graham, left-back Eddie McCreadie and defender Marvin Hinton completed a line-up which finished fifth in their first season back at the top. He'd go on to manage Manchester United and Scotland later in his career.

Tommy at Stamford Bridge with a giant bottle of champagne in May 1967.

Chelsea players preparing for their return to First Division football listen to their manager, Tommy Docherty, at a training session in Surrey in July 1963.

FOOTBALL
–STATS–

Tommy Docherty

Name: Thomas Henderson Docherty

Born: Glasgow, Scotland, 1928

Position: Wing-half

Chelsea Career: 1961-62

Playing Career: 1947–1961

Chelsea Appearances: 4

Chelsea Manager: 1961–1967

Scotland Appearances: 25

Goals: 1

Training Ground Tales

Chelsea players visiting Bournemouth for a golf break in March 1966. Left to right: Bobby Tambling, Peter Bonetti, physio Harry Medhurst, manager Tommy Docherty, Barry Bridges, John Hollins, Ron Harris, Eddie McCreadie, Ken Shellito and Allan Young. While Tommy got on well with players, he knew when to be strict with them as well. "I learnt from Tommy Docherty never to sit on the fence," said George Graham, who would go on to manage Arsenal. "A lot of players think they'll go into management and stay friends with everybody, but you have to make unpleasant decisions that will hurt people. If you don't like that, don't go into football management."

Barry Bridges and Derek Kevan pictured at the training ground in 1963. Barry, a striker who played upfront or on either wing, played for Chelsea for eight years from 1958 to 1966, making 205 appearances and scoring 93 goals. Kevan, though, made only seven appearances for The Blues in 1963.

While not always remembered for his tactics, Tommy was known for his innovative ideas to keep training fresh, such as making striker Tony Hateley wear a 21lb canvas waistcoat in November 1966.

—LEGENDS—

Ron "Chopper" Harris

No player has left his mark on the club as much as Ron Harris. "Chopper" made almost 800 appearances in a 19-year career for The Blues. Born in Hackney in 1944, he was simply one of the hardest, if not hardest, centre-halves to play the game. He was a natural leader and in 1967 he was the youngest ever skipper to lead out a side at the age of 22 in a FA Cup Final. Ron's game wasn't just about aggression – he was talented as well, even if his hard tackling did often spark controversy and red cards.

Two of Chopper's most legendary matches were the 1970 FA Cup Final and replay vs Leeds United, games regarded as two of the most physical of all time. Amid the carnage, Ron stood strong and one meaty tackle in the replay on Eddie Gray seemed to scare the life out of the winger, who was missing in action for the rest of the game. "Tommy Docherty, gave me a fantastic tip about man-marking," Chopper says. "He told me to larrup somebody in the first few minutes, and after that just to stay behind them and cough every now and then, to show them I was not too far away." Ron left for Brentford to be player-coach in 1980 after losing the captaincy to, ironically, a youngster – 18-year-old Ray Wilkins.

Chelsea defeat Everton 3-1 in a league match at The Bridge in September 1965. Everton's Alex Young gets some trademark close attention from Chopper.

Ron Harris in February 1964.

It's sweet dreams for Ron on his way home on the train to London from Manchester after his side's win over Leeds in the 1970 Cup Final at Old Trafford.

In my time, you would quite often play ankle deep in mud. You could let the forward get half a yard in front of you and could slide him and the spray would come up and you would take everything – the ball and him into the hoardings.

Ron Harris

A familiar sight as Ron gets his marching orders at Brighton during a 2-0 victory in the FA Cup third round in January 1973.

FOOTBALL
–STATS–

Ron Harris

Name: Ronald Edward Harris

Born: Hackney, 1944

Position: Centre-half

Playing Career: 1961-1983

Chelsea Career: 1961–1980

Club Appearances: 795

Goals: 14

Back Where We Belong

Docherty and the lads celebrate automatic promotion back to Division One after finishing second in Division Two in 1963, thanks to a nail-biting win at rivals Sunderland 1-0 and a 7-0 drubbing of Portsmouth at Stamford Bridge on the last day of the season. Bobby Tambling was the top scorer with 37 goals.

The Kings Of The King's Road

The 1960s was when footballers started to become the mega-rich superstars we know today. But as Greaves said, players during that time still had a close relationship with the fans that would seem unimaginable today. It was a game played by and watched by the working class. Here, legendary striker Bobby Tambling takes public transport to work from his home in Malden, Surrey, in February 1963. He was on a reported 60 quid a week.

Relaxing in a London café in April 1965, Left to right: Barry Bridges, Joe Fascione, John Hollins, Bert Murray and Marvin Hinton.

Up For The Cup

George Graham, John Hollins, Terry Venables and Chopper Harris are stunned after hearing they have been drawn against the holders Liverpool in the third round of the FA Cup in January 1966.

John Dempsey helps Peter Bonetti thwart a Forest attack at the City Ground in a 1-1 draw in November 1969.

–LEGENDS–

Peter Bonetti

If one player can nearly match Chopper's legendary status at the club, it's goalkeeper Peter Bonetti. "The Cat", as he was known because of his incredible agility and breath-taking saves, played for Chelsea for almost 20 years between 1960 and 1979. He left for a brief stint on a free to play in the North American Soccer League in 1975, making 21 appearances for the St Louis Stars. He returned to The Blues later that year and helped Eddie McCreadie's side gain promotion in 1977.

The biggest disappointment for Bonetti has to be his lack of England caps – he only won seven, a victim of playing in the same era as Gordon Banks and Peter Shilton. Unfortunately, his one World Cup appearance was a disaster, with England losing to West Germany 3-2 after being 2-0 up. But he kept over 200 clean sheets for Chelsea and is remembered for fine performances against Leeds in the 1970 FA Cup Final and the 1971 UEFA Cup Winners Cup Final against a strong Real Madrid. His saves helped Chelsea win 2-1. Pelé once called Peter one of the three greatest keepers he'd ever seen.

He kept Law in order!

DENIS LAW didn't look like £50,000-worth of footballer at Chelsea on Saturday. Billy McAdams, Manchester City's Irish international centre forward, is flabbergasted (left) as inside forward Law misses a sitter, and throws back his head in despair.

But Chelsea's eighteen-year-old Peter Bonetti, who cost them only the £20 signing-on fee, had a magnificent game in his first League match. And when Law did hit a good one (right), Bonetti made a great save to help Chelsea win.

BONETTI TAKING ON GUNNERS

The *Mirror* reports on Bonetti's league debut in 1960 against Manchester City, a game Chelsea won 3-0.

Peter Bonetti in training in May 1963.

95

Bonetti back at Stamford Bridge after a successful summer spell in America with the St Louis Stars in September 1975. It's a photo you're not likely to see Petr Cech posing for any time soon.

FOOTBALL
–STATS–

Peter Bonetti

Name: Peter Phillip Bonetti
Born: Putney, 1941
Position: Goalkeeper
Playing Career: 1960–1986
Chelsea Career: 1959–1979
Club Appearances: 729
Goals: 0
England Appearances: 7
Goals: 0

Things were often unpredictable when Chelsea took the field.

Peter Bonetti

Bonetti lays flat out during training in December 1969.

The Cat saves at the feet of Peter Lorimer in a 1-0 league victory over Leeds in November 1965.

The 1965 League Cup Final

Played in the days before the League Cup was held at Wembley, Docherty's Blues overcame a powerful, determined City side in a two-legged final. The first leg was at Stamford Bridge and Chelsea won 3-2 in a close game in which The Foxes came from behind twice. Tambling and Venables scored goals but the winner came from a jaw-dropping solo effort from Eddie McCreadie, who dribbled past several defenders before slotting past England's Gordon Banks. Some claim it is the best goal ever seen at Stamford Bridge. The second leg finished 0-0 at Filbert Street.

Terry Venables holds up the League Cup with Eddie McCreadie, John Mortimore, Marvin Hinton and John Hollins after beating Leicester City in the two-legged final.

The League Cup winning squad in August 1965. Left to right, back row: John Hollins, Allan Young, Bert Murray, Ken Shellito, Jim Barron, Peter Bonetti, Marvin Hinton, John Mortimore, Ron Harris and Peter Osgood. Front row: Bobby Tambling, George Graham, Jim McCalliog, Barry Bridges, Terry Venables, Peter Houseman and John Boyle.

Barry Bridges and Terry Venables hold up the
League Cup trophy in the dressing room.

–LEGENDS–

Terry Venables

Controversy has followed Venables throughout his career, and it was no different at Chelsea. He joined as an apprentice in 1957 and turned professional in 1960. He was skipper for a time and scored in that League Cup Final against Leicester City. But Terry was one of the eight players who broke a pre-match curfew in 1966, and his career at Stamford Bridge was never the same again. He fell out with gaffer Tommy Docherty and was sold to Spurs for £80,000.

El Tel flashes that familiar grin in September 1964.

FOOTBALL –STATS–

Terry Venables

Name: Terence Frederick Venables

Born: Dagenham, 1943

Position: Midfielder

Playing Career: 1960–1976

Chelsea Career: 1960–1966

Club Appearances: 237

Goals: 31

England Appearances: 2

Goals: 0

Terry Venables (lying on the left bench) gets treated by Harry Medhurst in 1965 for muscle problems, just 90 minutes after arriving at Heathrow Airport from playing in Europe. Also waiting for treatment are Peter Bonetti, Marvin Hinton, Bert Murray and Eddie McCreadie (on the right bench).

Tony Allen of Stoke City tackles Venables in May 1963. Chelsea lost the match 1-0.

Peter Osgood, Marvin Hinton, Barry Bridges, Terry Venables, John Hollins and Peter Bonetti pose at Stamford Bridge in April 1966.

Liverpool and Chelsea fans watch the FA Cup semi-final at Villa Park in March 1965. Liverpool won 2-0.

Stamford Bridge under water as a match with Sheffield United is called off in 1965.

–LEGENDS–

Peter Osgood

Chelsea's ability to find gems in their youth ranks during the 1950s and 1960s was remarkable. As if producing players such as Greaves, Venables and Harris wasn't enough, Osgood arrived on the scene to a phenomenal amount of hype in 1964 and would be crowned the King of Stamford Bridge by the fans. The striker scored twice on his debut against Wokingham in the League Cup and never looked back.

He hit the net 12 times on an end-of-season tour of Australia and was a regular in the first team by September 1965. One of his most famous goals came after a 60-yard run against Burnley. He narrowly missed out on the 1966 World Cup squad, and injury robbed him of a place in the 1967 Cockney Cup Final at Wembley, which Chelsea lost 2-1. He scored in both legs of the European Cup Winners' Cup Final against Real Madrid in 1971. He fell out with Dave Sexton in 1974 and was sold to Southampton, which shocked the fans. Sadly, Peter passed away in March 2006 after suffering a heart attack.

Peter Osgood in the boot room at Stamford Bridge, February 1966.

Osgood is challenged by Peter Storey of Arsenal during a Division One match at Stamford Bridge in September 1969. The Blues went on to win 3-0.

FOOTBALL
–STATS–

Peter Osgood

Name: Peter Leslie Osgood

Born: Windsor, 1947

Died: Slough, 2006

Position: Centre-forward

Playing Career: 1964–1979

Club Appearances: 380

Goals: 150

England Appearances: 4

Goals: 0

The Curfew Controversy

One of the biggest 'what ifs' in the history of Chelsea came in 1965. With two games to go and the club in the hunt for a league title, the wheels well and truly came off. Rumours had been circulating for months that the dressing room was split and that Venables and Docherty weren't getting on. Venables was accused of being disruptive, the whispers said, and was even guilty of changing tactics at the start of matches. The trouble came to a head when Venables and seven other players broke a 9pm curfew ahead of a game at Burnley, while on a trip to Blackpool. When the hotel night porter spilt the beans, Docherty blew his top and the players were sent home. A mixture of youth and reserve team players lost 6-2. The damage was done and a league title was lost.

The smiles hide the cracks: Tommy Docherty poses with the eight players he sent home after a night on the town in Blackpool.

George Graham, Barry Bridges and Bert Murray climb into a minibus at Euston Station on their way to Stamford Bridge.

The players before their match with Blackpool after manager Tommy Docherty had forgiven the curfew breakers. Left to right: John Hollins, Marvin Hinton, Joe Fascioni, George Graham, Tommy Docherty, Bert Murray, Terry Venables, Barry Bridges and Eddie McCreadie.

–LEGENDS–

Bobby Tambling

Some players are legends because of their reputation, others because of simple statistics. Bobby Tambling earns such plaudits thanks to being the club's all-time top scorer, with a storming 202 league and cup strikes in 370 appearances. It's a phenomenal scoring rate for a forward who stepped up to the plate and replaced another legend – Jimmy Greaves. Bobby joined as a junior in 1957 and made his debut aged 17 against West Ham, scoring the winner. He forged a fearsome partnership upfront with Barry Bridges, before switching to the left wing with the emergence of Peter Osgood. Fans were left wondering how many more goals he would have scored had he remained a forward. After 11 years at the club, he joined Crystal Palace in 1973.

Bobby Tambling in 1963.

Tambling in action during the 1966/7 season in a match against Villa. He scored five goals in a 6-2 Chelsea victory.

FOOTBALL
-STATS-

Bobby Tambling

Name: Robert Victor Tambling

Born: Storrington, Sussex, 1941

Position: Centre-forward

Playing Career: 1959–1979

Chelsea Career: 1958–1970

Club Appearances: 370

Goals: 202

England Appearances: 3

Goals: 1

The Fairs Cup

If the Premiership stars of today think they play too many matches, they should have been in the 1965/6 Chelsea side. As well as the three domestic competitions, they also got to the semi-finals of the Fairs Cup, in the days before there was a subs' bench. Chelsea's Fairs Cup run was eventful, to say the least. A 4-1 victory over Roma saw violence on and off the pitch. Roma fans ambushed the team bus and trouble on the pitch saw McCreadie sent off for throwing a punch. The return leg saw Roma move the match to a smaller ground with a more intimidating atmosphere, and fans threw rotten fruit and concrete at the Chelsea players. A victory over AC Milan was decided on a coin toss after finishing level. They then drew 2-2 with Barcelona after a two-legged semi-final, and were knocked out after another coin toss, which meant the replay would be held at the Nou Camp, where Chelsea lost 5-0. It was the start of the end for the Chelsea side of the early 1960s, with Docherty selling off the likes of Venables, Bridges and George Graham in the summer of 1966.

Chelsea take on Barcelona in the final at The Bridge.

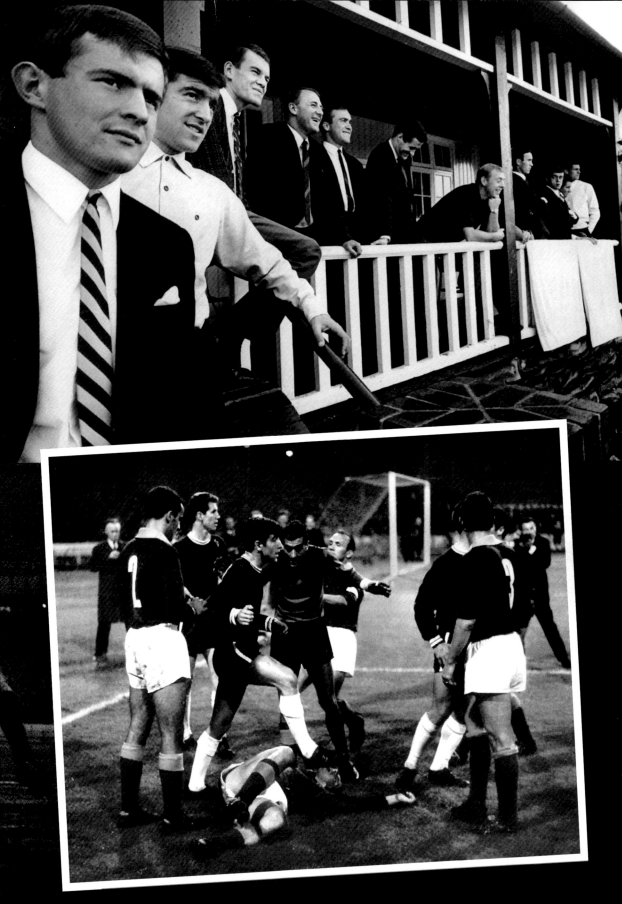

RIGHT: Chelsea players watch Roma training before they meet in the Fairs Cup. Left to right: John Hollins, Terry Venables, Eddie McCreadie, Tommy Docherty, Ron Harris, George Graham, Ken Shellito, Barry Bridges and Joe Fascione.

BELOW RIGHT: Terry Venables leaps to the defence of team-mate Eddie McCreadie by stepping over Roma's Leonardi. McCreadie was shown the red card after the incident.

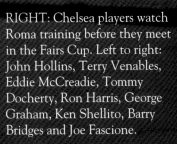

George Graham

George Graham in the dressing room at Stamford Bridge in August 1965. He joined in 1964 from Aston Villa for £5,950. His two years at the club were eventful: he scored 46 goals, was part of the League Cup winning team in 1965 and fell out with Docherty over that curfew.

Rebuilding The Bridge

The renovation of Stamford Bridge began in 1965. The terracing on the west side of The Bridge was replaced that year by the all-seater West Stand. Most of the West Stand consisted of rising ranks of wooden tip-up seats on iron frames, but seating at the very front was on concrete forms known as "the Benches". The old West Stand was demolished and replaced in 1998 with the current West Stand.

Tommy Docherty christens the centre spot of the Stamford Bridge pitch with champagne, watched by ground staff, before the start of the new season in August 1965.

Forest take on Chelsea at Stamford Bridge. Goalkeeper Peter Grummitt looks on as Peter Houseman (not in the picture) shoots wide of the post during a 1-0 defeat in February 1965.

The Cockney Cup Final

The 1967 FA Cup Final was unique for many reasons. It was the first contested between two London clubs but the real spice came in the line-ups, with ex-Chelsea stars Venables and Greaves playing for Spurs. "I didn't look forward to that final," Greaves said. "I was facing Chopper and he was the opponent I hated playing more than any other." Ron Harris was the youngest ever player to captain his side in the final in the history of the FA Cup, but he failed to inspire The Blues in a less than memorable final, which Chelsea lost 2-1. Thankfully, neither of the ex-Chelsea stars scored. Tambling netted an 85th minute consolation. "We had a young side and we just froze on the day," Chopper said.

Jimmy Greaves on the prowl during the final.

CHELSEA (Blue shirts, blue shorts)

1. PETER BONETTI 2. ALLAN HARRIS 3. EDDIE McCREADIE 4. JOHN HOLLINS 5. MARVIN HINTON 6. RON HARRIS (Captain) 7. CHARLIE COOKE 8. BOBBY TAMBLING 9. TOMMY BALDWIN 10. TONY HATELEY 11. JOHN BOYLE

TOTTENHAM HOTSPUR (White shirts, white shorts)

1. PAT JENNINGS 2. JOE KINNEAR 3. CYRIL KNOWLES 4. ALAN MULLERY 5. MIKE ENGLAND 6. DAVE MACKAY (Captain) 7. JIMMY ROBERTSON 8. JIMMY GREAVES 9. ALAN GILZEAN 10. TERRY VENABLES 11. FRANK SAUL

BELOW LEFT: Bobby Tambling watches as his boots are specially made ahead of the final.

BELOW: WAGS: 1960s style, as the Chelsea wives cry at the end of the semi-final vs Leeds in April 1967, which Chelsea won 1-0.

Dave Webb looks relaxed during an English League Division One match at Stamford Bridge against Leeds in January 1970, despite the final scoreline being 5-2 to Leeds. Chelsea played Leeds a remarkable six times that season – twice in the League Cup and twice in the FA Cup Final. Despite the heavy defeat in January, Webb and Chelsea got the last laugh with the Cup victory in April.

–LEGENDS–

Dave Webb

Despite being called porky during his career, Dave Webb was a commanding defender who joined the club from Southampton in 1968. He cemented his place in the hearts of Chelsea fans in the 1970 FA Cup Final. After a shocking performance at right-back marking Eddie Gray in the first match against Leeds, Dave Sexton shifted him to the centre of defence. He played a blinder in the replay and scored the winning goal, heading in an Ian Hutchinson throw-in during extra-time. Dave Webb just loved to play, wherever he was on the pitch. He scored a hat-trick playing upfront against Ipswich in 1968 and played in goal for one match, keeping a clean sheet against Ipswich in a 2-0 victory in 1971.

FOOTBALL –STATS–

Dave Webb

Name: David James Webb

Born: Stratford, London, 1946

Position: Defender, Centre-forward, Goalkeeper

Playing Career: 1963–1984

Chelsea Career: 1968–1974

Club Appearances: 299

Goals: 33

Chelsea Manager: 1993

Dave Sexton and Peter Osgood give Webb a short back and sides on their train journey back from Manchester after the FA Cup Final replay at Old Trafford.

Chelsea fans are frisked and their boots checked for steel toecaps before the match with Arsenal at Stamford Bridge in September 1969.

Young Chelsea fan Jimmy Tyler, who was mauled by a puma, meets his football heroes. Left to right: Ron Harris, Peter Osgood, David Webb, John Hollins and Marvin Hinton in December 1970.

Roy Stowers is allowed hospital leave to watch his team in the FA Cup tie against West Bromwich Albion in March 1969.

Sexton Takes Charge

Taking over from Docherty in 1967, Dave Sexton inherited a struggling side with plenty of talent. After signing the likes of Ian Hutchinson, he won the FA Cup in 1970 and European Cup Winners' Cup a year later, reaching the League Cup Final in 1972 against Stoke. But like Docherty before him, Sexton fell out with key players, this time Charlie Cooke, Osgood and Alan Hudson, who were sold during his spell in charge. He famously transfer-listed Osgood after a 3-2 defeat to Manchester United, claiming Osgood showed a lack of effort and even made him train with the youth team. He also stripped Ron Harris of the captaincy, handing it to Eddie McCreadie. Sexton was a quiet, thoughtful but tough manager.

He was regarded as a fine coach, who lacked the personal touch when it came to his players and had trouble communicating with them. In particular, it was claimed he had difficulty dealing with players who drank in the same pubs as the fans, which led to his setting an unsuccessful drinking ban at the club. A European Cup Winners' Cup trophy is evidence that while there is some truth in those stories, he could still motivate teams to victory. He was sacked in October 1974 with the side struggling after a 1-0 home defeat to Wolves. He had lost the dressing room. His decision to sell those star players set the club back years and prevented Chelsea from being one of the most dominant teams in football during the 1970s.

RIGHT: Sexton with Chairman Charles Pratt in October 1967.

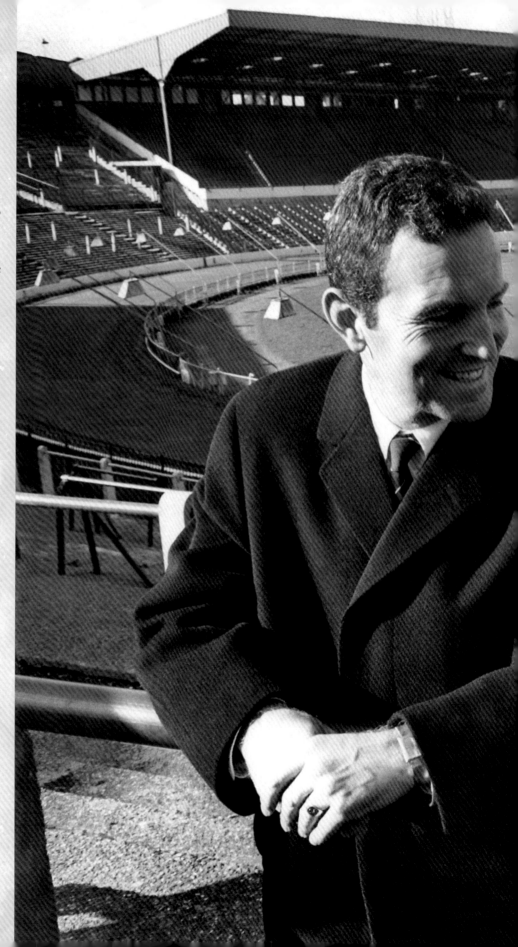

English managers, in Mexico to watch the 1970 World Cup, relax with a spot of golf. Left to right: Bobby Robson (Ipswich,) Dave Sexton (Chelsea), Alan Ashman (West Brom), Bertie Mee (Arsenal), watch Don Howe, Arsenal's assistant manager, practise his putting.

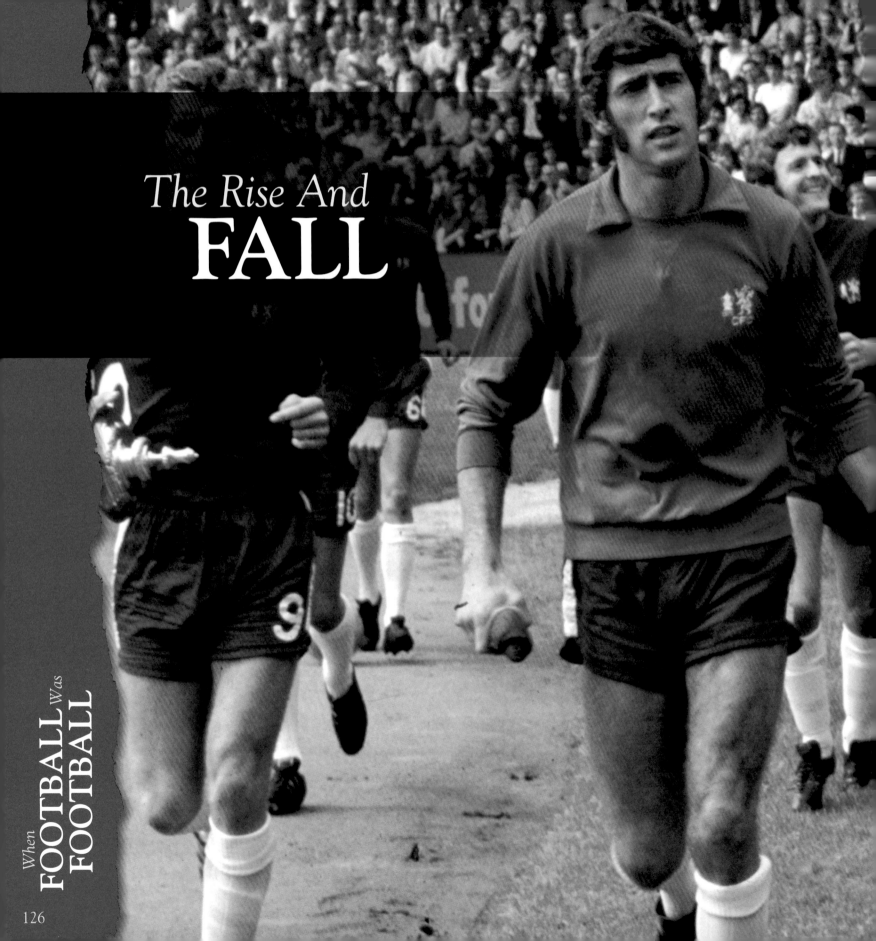

The Rise And
FALL

Peter Bonetti and Peter Houseman parade the FA Cup on a lap of honour during the Charity Shield match against Everton in August 1970. Everton won 2-1.

1970 Osgood and Hutchinson score 53 goals between them, helping the club finish third in the league and reach another FA Cup Final. They draw 2-2 with Leeds, winning the replay 2-1. **1971** Win the European Cup Winners' Cup against Real Madrid 2-1 **1971** Chelsea set two records in defence of the Cup Winners' Cup: a 21-0 aggregate win over Luxembourg side Jeunesse Hautcharage, which remains a record scoreline in European competition. The home leg score was a 13-0 home win, the biggest winning scoreline in Chelsea's history. But the team is knocked out of the competition by little-known Åtvidabergs FF. **1972** Lose the League Cup Final to Stoke City 2-1. **1972** The players record the now legendary song Blue Is The Colour. **1974** Dave Sexton sacked early into the season after a poor start. Ron Suart takes over. **1975** Chelsea relegated after finishing in 21st place. Ian Hutchinson is top scorer in the league with a paltry seven goals in a poor season all round in West London. **1975** Eddie McCreadie appointed manager and leads the side to promotion again in 1976/7. **1977** McCreadie quits following a contract dispute with chairman Brian Mears over a company car. Another ex-player is appointed, former right-back Ken Shellito. **1977** The club's debts stand at around £4 million. **1979** England's 1966 World Cup final hero Geoff Hurst becomes manager in September, with Bobby Gould as his assistant. The team scored in only three of their final 22 games that season.

Chelsea take on Leeds in the FA Cup Final on 11th April 1970. The Wembley pitch was in a state because the Horse of the Year Show had taken place there a week earlier.

The 1970 FA Cup Final

Dave Sexton's side won the oldest cup competition in the world after beating Leeds 2-1 in a replay, after the first game finished 2-2. In the first match, Peter Houseman scored with a low, 20-yard shot (which was fumbled by the keeper) and Ian Hutchinson nodded home a header in the 86th minute, just two minutes after Mick Jones had scored what looked like a winner for Leeds. Jones again gave Leeds the lead in the replay at Old Trafford, but Osgood equalized with 12 minutes to go and Dave Webb hit the winner in extra-time after a long throw from Hutchinson. But goals are not what the finals are remembered for. The games were brutal affairs, particularly the replay. Under modern rules, at least six of the players would have been sent off and most of the 22 booked. Ron Harris kicked lumps out of Eddie Gray (who had terrorized Chelsea's back-four in the first match), after just eight minutes, and Gray went AWOL for the rest of the match. Jack Charlton head-butted and delivered another nasty foul on Peter Osgood, and there were fights involving Norman Hunter, Hutchinson, McCreadie and Johnny Giles. A then record 32 million people watched the bedlam on TV.

Charlie Cooke crosses the ball, surrounded by Terry Cooper and John Giles of Leeds.

Chelsea fans queue for tickets for the replay.

Wearing a cup on his head became a familiar pose for Chopper, who's boarding a London-bound train with the FA Cup after the replay at Old Trafford.

Peter Bonetti and Tommy Baldwin celebrate in the bath.

The 1970 FA Cup Final

—LEGENDS—

Alan Hudson

Hudson was one of Chelsea's most popular players during the 1970s – and not just because of his flair in midfield. The playmaker was a local lad. Born and bred near the King's Road and rejected by Fulham as a schoolboy, Hudson was only prevented from making his debut at 16 by injury – the same reason why he missed the 1970 Cup Final. The likes of Charlie Cooke and Osgood fed off of Hudson's creativity and he helped them finish third in the league that season. He played a pivotal role in the 1971 European Cup Winners' Cup Final against Real Madrid but is one of those players who left Chelsea fans wondering "what if?". Another one to fall out with Dave Sexton, he was transfer-listed along with Osgood in January 1974 and joined Stoke for £240,000. He was just 22.

Alan with bride Maureen O' Doherty after their wedding in July 1971.

Peter Osgood and Hudson in December 1971.

FOOTBALL —STATS—

Alan Hudson

Name: Alan Anthony Hudson

Born: Chelsea, 1951

Position: Midfielder

Playing Career: 1968–1985

Chelsea Career: 1968–1974 & 1983–1984

Club Appearances: 189

Goals: 14

England Appearances: 2

Goals: 0

Hudson leads out the team at White Hart Lane in March 1971. Chelsea lost the match 2-1.

" We had a team at Chelsea that was a delight to watch. We were allowed to express ourselves with the ball. "

Alan Hudson

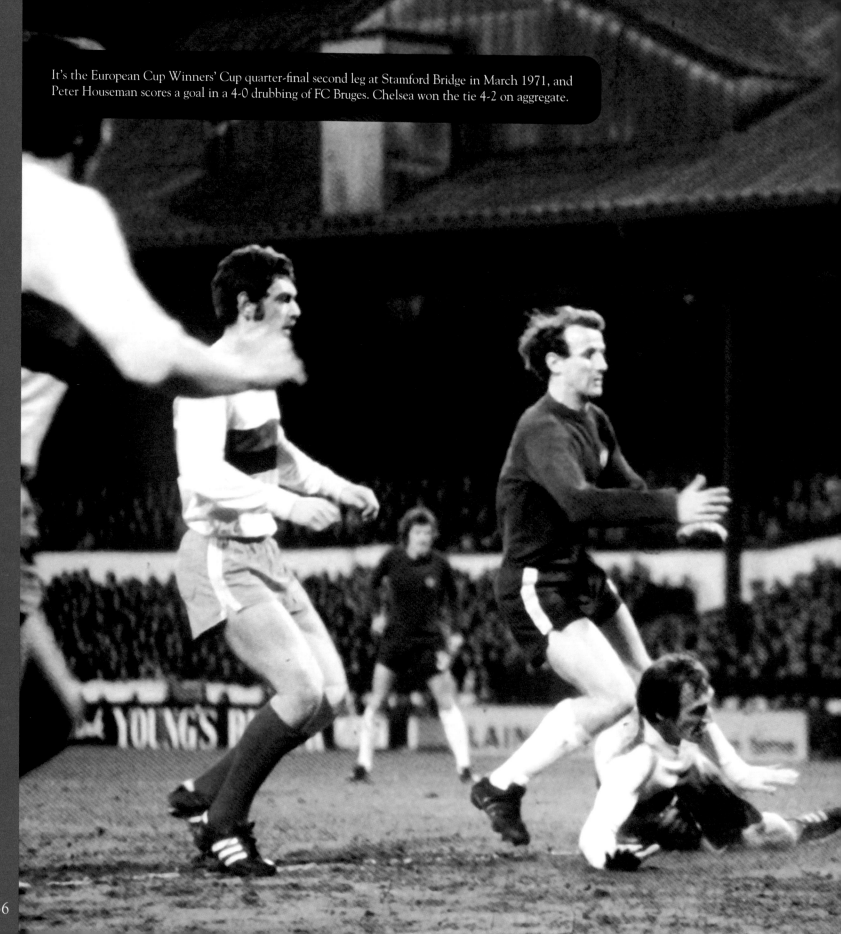

It's the European Cup Winners' Cup quarter-final second leg at Stamford Bridge in March 1971, and Peter Houseman scores a goal in a 4-0 drubbing of FC Bruges. Chelsea won the tie 4-2 on aggregate.

The Cup Winners' Cup

For all the criticism of Sexton's managerial style, he brought phenomenal success to Chelsea, winning two major trophies in two years. Victory in the European Cup Winners' Cup against Real Madrid in 1971 was his defining moment. The first game ended in a 1-1 draw before Chelsea won the trophy thanks to a 2-1 victory just two days later.

Chelsea embark on their victory parade after winning the European Cup Winners' Cup in May 1971.

The Blues started the match with real determination, scoring two goals in the first 40 minutes through defender John Dempsey (whose error while clearing the ball in the first game had resulted in Madrid's late equalizer) and Peter Osgood, who also netted the goal in the first match. But Chelsea mainly had Peter Bonetti to thank. The Cat's saves kept Real at bay, with one spectacular effort denying Zoco a clear goal in the final seconds of the match. It would take Chelsea another 27 years to win another European trophy.

Ron Harris leads the victory lap of honour at the Karaiskákis Stadium, Athens, Greece.

Ron Harris and Keith Weller bask in European glory.

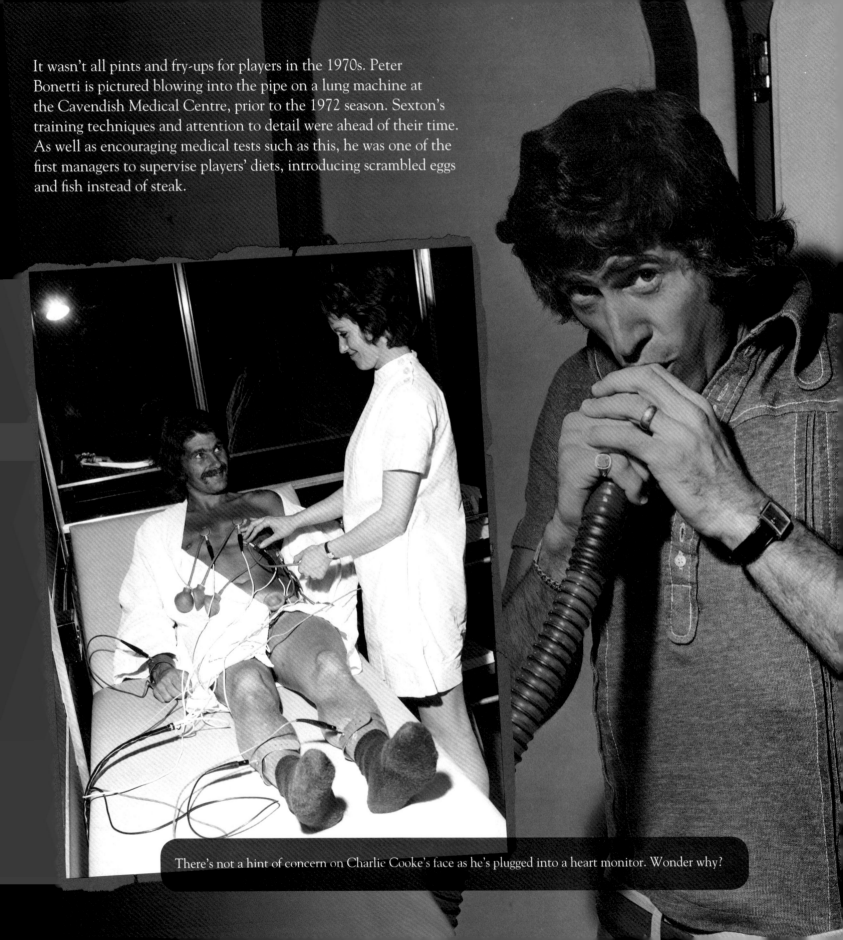

It wasn't all pints and fry-ups for players in the 1970s. Peter Bonetti is pictured blowing into the pipe on a lung machine at the Cavendish Medical Centre, prior to the 1972 season. Sexton's training techniques and attention to detail were ahead of their time. As well as encouraging medical tests such as this, he was one of the first managers to supervise players' diets, introducing scrambled eggs and fish instead of steak.

There's not a hint of concern on Charlie Cooke's face as he's plugged into a heart monitor. Wonder why?

Chelsea taking on West Ham in a league match at Stamford Bridge in September 1972. West Ham and England legend Bobby Moore tussles with Chris Garland for the ball. A battling forward, Garland made 114 appearances for Chelsea, scoring 31 goals. His most important two came in the League Cup semi-finals against Spurs in 1972.

21-0 Just For The Record

It's still a Chelsea record – a crushing 21-0 victory over Luxembourg side Jeunesse Hautcharage in the European Cup Winners' Cup in September 1971. Peter Osgood bagged eight of them over the two legs, five of them in the second match. Tommy Baldwin also got a hat-trick in the second leg. The first leg away from home finished 8-0 to The Blues, while at Stamford Bridge the score was a whopping 13-0.

To add insult to injury, the minnows' keeper took a
nasty cut to the face during the match.

The League Cup Final

Winning two cups in 1970 and 1971 and a high league finish meant Chelsea were the red-hot favourites to lift the League Cup when they clashed with Stoke in March 1972. But City, with England legend Gordon Banks in goal, were vying for their first-ever trophy and caused a major upset, winning 2-1 in front of 100,000 fans. Peter Osgood netted Chelsea's goal. It was the beginning of the end of Sexton's team, and Chelsea's golden era would soon come to an end.

Alan Hudson weaves his way through the Stoke defence.

Gordon Banks clears as Peter Osgood looks on.

Blue Is The Colour

One good thing came out of that final, even if Chelsea lost the game. The team recorded 'Blue Is The Colour', a song that is still a club anthem today. Recorded on Penny Farthing Records, it reached No. 5 in the charts in 1972. Tommy Baldwin, Peter Bonetti, Charlie Cooke, John Dempsey, Ron Harris, Marvin Hinton, John Hollins, Peter Houseman, Alan Hudson, Steve Kember, Eddie McCreadie, Paddy Mulligan, Peter Osgood and Dave Webb sang on the track. The song is so popular it has been adopted by teams in Canada and the former Czechoslovakia, and was even used by the Conservative Party in 1979 as part of the campaign that ushered Margaret Thatcher into power.

Chelsea's Got Talent: the squad recording the track in Highbury.

Right to left: Steve Kember, Dave Webb, Charlie Cooke and Paddy Mulligan sing their hearts out.

Celebrities flocked to The Bridge during the 1960s and 1970s to see Chelsea's flamboyant side. Among them were Richard Attenborough, Michael Caine, Steve McQueen and Raquel Welch, who attended a match against Leicester City in 1972 with Jimmy Hill.

The New East Stand

Construction of the new East Stand was finished in time for the opening game of the 1974 season against Carlisle United. The stand seated 11,280 and cost £2 million, partly due to a shortage of materials and a builders' strike. It almost ruined the club. It was meant to be the first phase of the redevelopment of the whole ground, but financial difficulties meant the stadium wasn't properly redeveloped until the 1990s. The East Stand's three tiers are still in place at Stamford Bridge today.

—LEGENDS—

Ian Hutchinson in 1969 before a match with Spurs.

Ian Hutchinson

Ian was a perfect foil for his more gifted partner upfront, Peter Osgood. Chelsea is the only club he played for, but injury seriously hindered the number of his appearances. When he did play, he brought a new dimension to the skilful Chelsea side. He was physical, had a sweet touch and one of the strongest long throws football has ever seen. One of his throws was measured at 112 feet, and on his debut they were so powerful they reached the other side of the penalty area. Another caused so much confusion that Ipswich scored an own goal.

Hutchinson and Osgood scored 53 goals between them in 1970, the season Chelsea won the FA Cup. In that game, it was his flick-on that set up Peter Houseman for Chelsea's first equalizer, and he headed in the second equalizer despite limping after a heavy challenge from Norman Hunter. Yet another long throw would be headed in by Dave Webb to win the Cup. Hutchinson would quite simply scrap for everything and was a talisman to the players around him. He was a great servant to Chelsea but his body just wasn't able to cope with the pressures of modern football. He suffered two broken legs, a broken arm, a broken toe and persistent knee trouble, which denied him a place in the Cup Winners' Cup run in 1972 and meant he played only four times in the 1972/3 season. He retired in July 1976 aged 27. Ian died in 2002 after a long illness.

Recovering from a broken leg in January 1972,
Hutchinson practises one of his trademark long throws.

FOOTBALL
–STATS–

Ian Hutchinson

Name: Ian Hutchinson

Born: Derby, 1948

Died: 2002

Position: Centre-forward

Playing Career: 1968–1976

Chelsea Career: 1968–1976

Club Appearances: 144

Goals: 58

At Home With Chelsea

There was no media training in the 1970s and players such as Bonetti, pictured were much more relaxed about showing a glimpse of their personal lives away from the pitch.

Bonetti and his family show off their caravan in December 1974.

Ian Hutchinson, who had injured his back, and Micky Droy, who was nursing an injured left groin, taking time out in January 1974.

Charlie Cooke poses in 1972.

–LEGENDS–

Charlie Cooke

A skilful winger from Scotland, Charlie had two spells at the club in the 1960s and 1970s. He first signed in April 1966 from Dundee for a then record £72,000 and went on to take Venables' place in the side, making his debut in the Fairs Cup against Barcelona. His league debut came the following season against West Ham and it was a memorable one – he turned Bobby Moore inside out and scored. Another player Sexton inexplicably shipped out, he was sold to Crystal Palace in 1972, but returned in 1974 to a very different club. The rot was setting in and the side was relegated in 1975. Cooke's experience proved vital though for Eddie McCreadie, who was now manager, and he was a vital cog in a young Chelsea side's promotion back to the top flight in 1977. He also earned 16 caps for Scotland before moving to America in 1978 to play in the now defunct NASL.

Charlie is challenged by John Robson of Derby County in 1970.

FOOTBALL
-STATS-
Charlie Cooke

Name: Charles Cooke

Born: St Monans, Scotland, 1942

Position: Winger

Playing Career: 1960–1985

Chelsea Career: 1966–1972 & 1974–1978

Club Appearances: 373

Goals: 30

Scotland Appearances: 16

Goals: 0

Trouble Ahead

A team on the decline: Chelsea were getting a bad reputation off the pitch as well as on it. Trouble was regularly flaring at matches, particularly if the opposition were Millwall or West Ham. Pictured is a League Division One match at Stamford Bridge fans in the crowd attempt to climb over the fence as police keep watch during a 1-1 draw with The Hammers in December 1974.

Tempers flare at The Bridge in 1977.

159

—LEGENDS—

Ray Wilkins

Another product of the youth team, "Butch" Wilkins is a player who is still associated with the club today. Chelsea were his boyhood club and he joined as an apprentice with his brothers Graham and Stephen, making his debut against Norwich in 1973. When Eddie McCreadie took over in 1975, and following relegation to Division Two, Wilkins was named skipper at the age of 18, taking over from Ron Harris. He was a pin-up for a generation of teenage girls, but, more importantly, a lynchpin in midfield who marshalled a young squad that won promotion in 1977. He was named Chelsea's Player Of The Year in 1976 and 1977.

Often called "The Crab" and slated because of his sideways passes, he left for Manchester United in 1979 after McCreadie left and the Red Devils offered £800,000 for his signature – massive money for a club in Chelsea's perilous financial position. He rejoined Chelsea under Gianluca Vialli in 2000 and returned again in 2008 to be assistant first-team coach, a role he still holds today. He's been caretaker manager twice during his time at the club. Butch was also famously the voice in a series of Tango soft drink adverts in the 1990s.

LEFT: Poster boy Wilkins in July 1976.

Wilkins looks cheesed off as Chelsea slump to a 3-1 defeat at Fulham (a club he would later go on to manage) in the rain in April 1977.

FOOTBALL
-STATS-
Ray Wilkins

Name: Raymond Colin Wilkins

Born: Hillingdon, 1956

Position: Central Midfielder

Playing Career: 1973–1997

Chelsea Career: 1973–1979

Club Appearances: 198

Goals: 34

England Appearances: 84

Goals: 3

Eddie McCreadie

A talented, attacking full-back, Eddie made 410 appearances for Chelsea as a player, scoring five goals. He was part of the Kings Of The King's Road side of the 1960s and 1970s, and scored the winner in the first leg of the 1965 League Cup Final against Leicester after a jaw-dropping 60-yard run. He was also in the 1970 and 1972 Cup Final sides. A Scotland international who won 23 caps, he retired in 1973 and joined the coaching staff at The Bridge. He was named gaffer in April 1975, too late to prevent relegation to Division Two, but he rebuilt the side, filled it with young players like Wilkins and won promotion back to the top flight in 1977. His reason for resigning after winning promotion was a curious one – he wanted a company car. Chairman Brian Mears said no, and the Scot was gone. Even when Mears gave in and offered the motor, McCreadie refused to change his mind on principle and left England for the North American Soccer League. He still lives in America.

Chelsea training under the watchful eye of McCreadie before a crucial relegation battle at Stamford Bridge in April 1975.

A concerned McCreadie examines the surface water on the pitch at Stamford Bridge with a groundsman in February 1977.

FOOTBALL
–STATS–

Micky Droy

Name: Micky Droy

Born: Highbury, 1951

Position: Central defender

Playing Career: 1970–1987

Chelsea Career: 1970–1985

Club Appearances: 313

Goals: 19

Two of Eddie's key players, Micky Droy and Gary Locke, get ready for kick-off at the start of their FA Cup fifth round tie with Crystal Palace in February 1976. Chelsea lost 3-2. Centre-half Droy spent 15 years at Chelsea between 1970 and 1985. Droy didn't mess about – a no nonsense defender, he arrived just after Chelsea's success in the early 1970s, just as the club was falling into decline on and off the pitch. He was Chelsea's Player Of The Year in 1978.

Battle For The BRIDGE

WELCOME TO STAMFO

| MATCH NO | SENIOR CITIZENS | £2·00 | £2·00 | £2·0 |
| 1 | £1·25 | CHILDREN UNDER 14 | | |

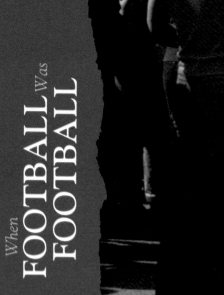

O BRIDGE

£2·00

CHELSEA FOOTBALL CLUB

Chelsea fans make their way into the stadium in August 1980.

1981 Fans invade the pitch protesting against chairman Brian Mears after a 2-0 home defeat to Notts County. Mears resigns as chairman. One of his last actions is to appoint John Neal as manager. **1981/2** Colin Pates is ever present. **1982** Chelsea Football & Athletic Company is bought by former Oldham Athletic chairman Ken Bates for £1. **1983** John Neal signs Kerry Dixon from Reading, winger Pat Nevin from Clyde, midfielder Nigel Spackman from Bournemouth and goalkeeper Eddie Niedzwiecki from Wrexham, all for a combined fee of under £500,000. **1984** Promoted back to the First Division as Champions. **1985** Finish sixth and lose 5-2 to Sunderland in the League Cup semi-final. Ex-Chelsea winger Clive Walker inspires his team to a 3-2 win at Stamford Bridge to seal a 5-2 aggregate win for Sunderland. **1985** Neal retires at the end of the season due to ill health and is replaced by Hollins. **1986** Win Full Members Cup, beating Manchester City 5-4, thanks to a David Speedie hat-trick and in spite of the opposition fighting back from 1-5 down. **1988** Hollins sacked in March with the side again in relegation trouble. Bobby Campbell takes over but cannot prevent Chelsea's relegation via the short-lived play-off system with a loss to Middlesbrough, a match that is marred by crowd trouble. The Bridge's terraces are closed for six games as punishment. **1989** Promoted as Second Division champions with 99 points, 17 points clear of nearest rivals Manchester City. **1990** Win Full Members Cup, beating Middlesbrough and finish fifth in the league.

Serbian goalkeeper Petar Borota doesn't know which boots to wear on QPR's newly installed Astroturf in 1981. Petar made 114 appearances for Chelsea between 1979 and 1982.

Mears Out, Bates In

Brian Mears is one of the most controversial characters in the history of Chelsea. It was his family who formed the club in 1905, and his first match was the Dynamo Moscow friendly in 1945. His father, Joe Mears, was chairman of the club, but died in 1966; Brian took over in 1969. Football was a glamorous game and Chelsea was a glamorous club, and Mears loved the King's Road lifestyle. With his fur coats and personalized number plates, he often looked more stylish than the players and he played host to many of the celebrities who watched Chelsea during the time. Mears' decision to renovate The Bridge during an economic meltdown was questioned: the rebuilding cost millions and drove the club deeper into crisis. With no money to buy players and tension on the terraces, the club was several million pounds in debt by 1981. Mears had also sold the freehold of the ground to a property developer. On the pitch, the club had failed badly with England legend Geoff Hurst as manager. Mears was out of his depth and the fans knew it, and a 2-0 defeat at home to Notts County was the final straw. Supporters invaded the pitch in protest. He stepped down and sold the club to Ken Bates for £1 in 1982.

Brian Mears in 1974.

PAGE 30   DAILY MIRROR, Tuesday, December 6, 1983

FRANK McGHEE

Down on the farm with Ken, the common man

KEN BATES, the flamboyant millionaire who likes to see his life as a crusade for Chelsea, has a short answer for anyone who suspects him of less admirable motives.

MAN OF PROPERTY: Chelsea chairman Ken Bates in front of his Buckinghamshire mansion.

'I have given Chelsea back to the fans'

FARMER: Bates rounds up his pedigree Friesians on his 300-acre estate.

Pictures: MIKE MALONEY

Ken Bates speaks to 10,000 Chelsea fans who went to Grimsby in May 1984 to celebrate the side's promotion back to the top flight.

Ken addresses the crowd during a Division One clash at Stamford Bridge in the 1985/6 season. Chelsea beat Everton 2-1.

Ken Bates

You know where you stand with Ken Bates. One of the most outspoken characters in the history of football, his no-nonsense approach to the sport and life meant he has as many enemies as friends. But his impact on Chelsea was phenomenal. After buying the club for £1, he cleared the debts and despite one or two hiccups along the way, started The Blues on the path to the glory they enjoy now. Born in 1931 in Ealing, he was brought up by his grandparents and made his money in the haulage industry, before moving into concrete, quarrying and dairy farming. He was chairman at Oldham for five years in the 1970s, but it was in West London where he made his name. He fought a long, gruelling battle to win back the freehold for Chelsea, battled to rid the club of its hooligan problem and publicly backed the team's first black player, Paul Canoville, who had been racially abused by sections of the crowd. That infamous white beard was in charge for 21 years. Many people hated his methods, and he even banned Ron Harris and Peter Osgood at one point for slating him over how he ran the club. He didn't always cover himself in glory, calling Matthew Harding an evil man after his death and once labelled Aston Villa a "two bob side". But he was Chelsea's most successful owner until he sold the club to Roman Abramovich in 2003. Thanks to Ken's redevelopment work, Stamford Bridge is now one of the top stadiums in the country. He is now chairman of Leeds United.

John Neal

While Chelsea fans were rightly chanting for Mears' resignation in 1981, in hindsight, they should have added a thank you for John Neal as they showed him the door – because the one thing Mears did do right was to appoint the former Wrexham and Boro manager. The club was a mess when Neal took over. They narrowly avoided relegation to the Third Division in 1983, but then things started to come together. Neal made shrewd signings, including David Speedie, Kerry Dixon, Pat Nevin, Nigel Spackman and Eddie Niedzwiecki for less than £500,000 combined. In 1984, his side went up as Second Division champions. The following two seasons they finished sixth in the league. But once again, with dominance in sight, it all went wrong. Neal had heart surgery in 1986 and was forced to retire.

John Neal takes over in 1981.

John Neal with his ground staff at Stamford Bridge in January 1985.

An FA Cup fifth round tie at The Bridge in February 1982. Liverpool's Alan Hansen is tackled by Colin Lee. Chelsea won the match 2-0, causing quite an upset, as The Blues were in Division Two at the time and Liverpool went on to win the league that year.

–LEGENDS–

Kerry Dixon

John Neal noticed several things about Kerry Dixon when he was playing for Reading. He had impressive pace for a tall striker, could use both feet and had a good header on him. The most noticeable feature, though, was his goal-scoring record of almost a goal every two games. Neal signed him for £150,000 (a price Ken Bates was rumoured to think was too much) with an additional £25,000 on top if he ever played for England, which he did, scoring four goals in eight caps.

His partnership with the diminutive Scot David Speedie is one of the most legendary in the club's history – brilliant on the pitch together, although they sometimes didn't click with each other off it. He scored 70 goals in his first 101 games, but torn stomach muscles in 1986 robbed him of some of his pace and form, and he was dropped from the squad and was nearly sold to Arsenal, until Bates stepped in. The club was relegated in 1988, which Dixon actually benefited from. He found his scoring boots again and scored 25 goals as The Blues won the title. He claimed another 26 goals the following season back in the top flight. He is second behind Bobby Tambling in the club's all-time goalscorer list.

FOOTBALL
–STATS–

Kerry Dixon

Name: Kerry Michael Dixon

Born: Luton, 1961

Position: Centre-forward

Playing Career: 1980–1997

Chelsea Career: 1983–1992

Club Appearances: 420

Goals: 193

England Appearances: 8

Goals: 4

Kerry in action, 1984.

Back At The Top

Chelsea's 1984 promotion team was all about goals. Kerry Dixon got 36 of them in all competitions, and they started the season with a 5-0 win over Derby, and had the same scoreline in their last home game against Leeds. They beat Kevin Keegan's Newcastle 4-0, beat Swansea 6-1 and won 5-3 at Fulham. Mickey Thomas was signed to play on the wing when the team's form took a dip around Christmas, and Chelsea didn't lose a single game after that.

Dixon scoring one of his three goals in a 5-0 win against Leeds in April 1984 as The Blues secure promotion.

" *Managing to throw Ken Bates in the bath after winning promotion was a great moment.*

Kerry Dixon "

The fans are on the pitch at The Bridge – but this time they're celebrating.

The Blues took 10,000 fans to Grimsby for the last game of the season for the mother of all parties in May 1984. Chelsea won 1-0.

175

—LEGENDS—

Pat Nevin

John Neal signed Pat Nevin from Clyde in the summer of 1983. The Scotland international went on to supply pinpoint crosses and regularly fooled full-backs for five years, before leaving for Everton. But he wasn't just a creator. He scored 14 goals in his first season and his best performance that year was during a 4-0 drubbing of Newcastle. Nevin shone in the top flight and steered the club towards the Milk Cup Final in 1985. He set up three goals in the quarter-final vs Sheffield Wednesday, as Chelsea came back from 3-0 down to draw 4-4. He was voted Player Of The Year twice and was sold to Everton only when the club was relegated by Middlesbrough in the ill-fated play-offs in 1988.

During the rest of his career, however, he never reached the dizzy heights he did at Chelsea, and is now a radio broadcaster and analyst. Long before the controversy over the *Guardian* reading Graham Le Saux, Nevin was not your average footballer. He has an arts degree and appeared in the music journal *NME* because of his passion for bands such as Joy Division.

Nevin goes for the popstar look in February 1985.

At home with Pat Nevin and his extensive record collection.

Pat Nevin lines up with the Charlton wall in October 1983. Chelsea won the game 3-2.

FOOTBALL
-STATS-

Pat Nevin

Name: Patrick Kevin Francis Michael Nevin

Born: Glasgow, 1963

Position: Winger

Playing Career: 1981–2000

Chelsea Career: 1983–1988

Club Appearances: 242

Goals: 45

Scotland Appearances: 28

Goals: 5

The glamour of Division One football: construction work at The Bridge doesn't stop Chelsea taking on Fulham in 1984.

Nigel Spackman in action for Chelsea against Ipswich at The Bridge in 1986. Another of Neal's 1983 signings, Spackman was a hard-working midfielder who scored on his debut in a 5-0 rout of Derby County. He made 267 appearances, scoring 14 goals. But along with several other players, he fell out with Neal's successor, John Hollins, and was sold to Liverpool in 1987, where he was a key part of a Liverpool side that pundits claimed played "total football". He spent another four years at The Bridge after rejoining in 1992.

Steady Eddie

A winning team needs a keeper
you can rely on and Niedzwiecki,
a Welshman with Polish roots,
was just that. He made 175
appearances for The Blues but was
forced to retire at the age of 28
due to injury. He was a coach at
Chelsea in the 1990s, but left in
2000 when Claudio Ranieri was
named manager. He now coaches at
Manchester City.

RIGHT: Eddie Niedzwiecki shouts orders to
his defence against Spurs in November 1984.

BELOW: Eddie leaps to save against Watford
in March 1985.

Darkness Descends

One of the darkest days during the 1980s for Chelsea was the 1985 Milk Cup semi-final defeat to Sunderland on 4th March 1985. Chelsea lost 2-3 (5-2 on aggregate), but the match was irrelevant compared to what was happening in the stands. The pitch was invaded, seats ripped up and missiles thrown. Mounted police stormed the pitch in one of the worst examples of football violence that decade. Everything that could go wrong that night did, with even David Speedie getting sent off and former Blue Clive Walker scoring two goals. Walker also crossed for the strangest of goals – Colin West nodded home as four policemen chased a hooligan across the penalty box. The fighting continued in the King's Road after the final whistle, and Chelsea were condemned in the press the next day. Chelsea's hooligan problems needed a solution – and Ken Bates thought he had one.

Ripped out seats litter the pitch.

An Electric Personality

Ken Bates' no-nonsense approach shocked pretty much everyone when he announced his solution to the hooligan problem at The Bridge. He wanted to install electric fences. He'd got the idea from working on his dairy farm – he used them to control his cattle. Bates clashed with the Greater London Council over the fence and even gave a personal demonstration that to touch

it wasn't life threatening, claiming it would only give you a burn mark on the finger. He was angered by the media's rejection of his idea, but in the end he never actually switched it on.

Mirror Sport

Tuesday, April 23, 1985   No. 25,244
Telephone: (STD Code: 01)—353 0246

EVANS: Changes

Luton's plastic plans

By HARRY MILLER

LUTON are planning to lay an artificial pitch as part of a £1 million facelift to their antiquated Kenilworth Road ground.

The synthetic surface, at a cost of around £250,000, will be put down this summer.

Queens Park Rangers were the pathfinders for artificial pitches in Europe. Their surface has generally been accepted this season after heavy initial criticism.

Luton chairman David Evans said: "You wouldn't expect Steve Davis to play snooker on an uneven table with bumpy cushions. Quality players should have a quality surface."

The Hatters won the very first game on Queens Park Rangers' plastic pitch in August 1981 and have won on each Loftus Road visit since.

Evans added: "Frankly, I don't know of many worse grounds than Kenilworth Road. We must make improvements."

These include 35 executive boxes, cover at the Kenilworth Road end and a family enclosure.

Luton also want to improve a team that is moving spiritedly away from the relegation zone.

GLC threat to pull plug on Chelsea

POWER STRUGGLE

WONDER BOY FOR SPURS

TOTTENHAM are set to sign Wonder Boy Sean Murray writes Harry Harris.

The 14-year-old midfield player from Newcastle, described by many as the hottest schoolboy prospect in the country, has been closely watched by Everton, Manchester United, Arsenal and Liverpool for several months.

Murray, an English schoolboy international, will follow in the footsteps of Mike Hazard, plucked from the north-west nearly 10 years ago and developed into one of the First Division's most talented midfielders.

His decision to move south will prove a great capture for the Spurs scouts.

BATES: On the offensive

CHELSEA chairman Ken Bates last night refused to back down over the use of an electrified fence at Stamford Bridge.

The Greater London Council have given him an ultimatum that if he goes ahead and switches on the fence, they will take out an injunction closing the ground and halting Saturday's match with Tottenham.

But the sparks flew as Bates hit back: "Why all this sudden compassion for the hooligans?

"Just a few weeks ago the whole nation was up in arms about these thugs attacking innocent people and driving them away from the game.

"Now there's all this concern that a few soccer hooligans might get their fingers burnt trying to scale the fences at Stamford Bridge.

"Many people have stopped me in the street and written me letters to say that they are in favour of this fence.

"But I've always said that if it is proven to be illegal then it will not go up. If it is legal, it will go up."

A GLC spokesman said: "Under the general safety certificate issued for Stamford

'So what if a few thugs get their fingers burned' — KEN BATES

By HARRY HARRIS

Bridge on February 13, Chelsea cannot make alterations to the stadium regarding such things as electricity, heating, lighting, and ventilation, without the written consent of the Council.

"We've ordered Chelsea to stop work and given them 24 hours to consider their position. If they decide not to co-operate with us, we will think about issuing a court injunction. Our lawyers are working on it.

"But, at the moment, we're hoping that Chelsea will respond positively to our recommendations."

As an alternative to caging in fans the FA yesterday suggested the use of see-through plastic screens.

Secretary Ted Croker has inspected the plastic squash court in use at Wembley Conference Centre for this week's British Open Championship and plans an outdoor test of the same material at Wembley.

Liverpool meanwhile have decided not to allocate seats to Chelsea supporters for their game at Anfield a week on Saturday in an attempt to avert trouble.

HOW TO HURT THE BULLIES—Page 30

Exchange all your bills for one easy monthly payment

CREDIT CARD ACCOUNT

PAY OUT LESS   £200   PAYMENT SLIP ONE PAYMENT ONLY £100

ONLY WE GIVE YOU YOUR FIRST MONTHLY PAYMENT FREE and there is nothing to pay for 60 days after you receive your cheque

PLUS FREE LIFE INSURANCE AT NO EXTRA COST!

Why pay more?

ANY PURPOSE QUICK PERSONAL SERVICE £2000-£20000

LOOK AT THESE BENEFITS!
- IMMEDIATE DECISION GIVEN
- HOME IMPROVEMENTS WITH FULL TAX RELIEF
- A SECURED LOAN FACILITY
- SELF EMPLOYED WELCOME (no accounts required)
- WRITTEN QUOTATIONS
- EARLY SETTLEMENT REBATES
- LICENSED LENDERS & BROKERS

You SAVE £153·18

FRIENDLY SERVICE Just dial 100 and ask for FREEPHONE LOAN PLAN we pay for the call

ANDY CAPP   by Reg Smythe

© The Daily Mirror Newspapers, Ltd., 1985

Fans celebrating Chelsea beating Southampton 2-0 in September 1985, thankfully able to grab the fence with no danger of being shocked.

The Full Members Cup

The Blues got some positive press after the Full Members Cup Final against Manchester City in March 1986. The competition was the brainchild of Ken Bates a year earlier. Exclusively designed for league clubs in a bid to compensate for the lack of European football in England while clubs were banned after the Heysel disaster, it lasted only seven years and isn't missed in the slightest. But the first final in 1986 between Chelsea and City was a belter, and one of the best matches to ever be played at Wembley. A crowd of 68,000 watched Chelsea win 5-4, thanks to two goals from Colin Lee and a David Speedie hat-trick, but only by the skin of their teeth, after City came back from 5-1 down.

Colin Lee and Speedie show
off the Full Members Cup.

David Speedie scores.

–LEGENDS–

David Speedie

While sometimes chalk and cheese off the pitch, Kerry Dixon and David Speedie understood each other on it. Speedie's attitude, spirit and work-rate made it impossible not to appreciate the Scottish striker. Another of Neal's masterstroke signings, this time from Darlington for £80,000 in 1982, his Full Members Cup hat-trick was the first at Wembley since Geoff Hurst's in the 1966 World Cup Final. He scored two on his debut against Oldham and helped keep the club in the Second Division in his first season. His spell at Chelsea really took off, though, with the arrival of Dixon. Ask most football fans to name a 1980s Chelsea striker and they'll most likely say Dixon, but Speedie's goals and tenacity were also vital in restoring pride to the West London club. Like many players, he fell out with manager John Hollins and left for Coventry in 1987.

Speedie scoring against Luton in a 1-0 victory in January 1986.

David Speedie

Name: David Robert Speedie

Born: Glenrothes, Scotland, 1960

Position: Centre-forward

Playing Career: 1978–1994

Chelsea Career: 1982–1987

Club Appearances: 205

Goals: 64

Scotland Appearances: 10

Goals: 0

Ken Bates and Hollins watching Chelsea play Oxford in March 1988, shortly before Hollins was sacked.

RIGHT: Hollins playing for Chelsea against Ricardo Villa and Spurs.

John Hollins

There are two sides to the John Hollins story. There's Hollins the player, a young hard-working midfielder with a ton of drive and energy who made his debut against Swindon when he was only 17 and went on to rack up nearly 600 appearances for the club. He scored 17 goals in the 1971/2 season and played in a consecutive 167 club matches, which is a club record. Then there's Hollins the gaffer. Appointed coach after his second playing stint in West London in 1984, he took over as manager after John Neal retired. Although he won that Full Members Cup Final against Manchester City, he fell out with key players such as Speedie and Nigel Spackman. Form dipped and he was sacked in March 1988, with the club struggling without a win in four months. It's safe to say most fans prefer to remember just one Hollins.

FOOTBALL
–STATS–
John Hollins

Name: John William Hollins

Born: Guildford, 1946

Position: Midfielder, Centre-half

Playing Career: 1963–1984

Chelsea Career: 1963–1975 & 1983–1984

Club Appearances: 592

Goals: 64

Chelsea Manager: 1985-88

England Appearances: 1

Goals: 0

Micky Hazard holds off Newcastle's Peter Beardsley in April 1986.

Bobby Campbell and the bench look on as another chance goes begging.

Down But Not Out

Bobby Campbell took over from Hollins but he wasn't instantly able to stop the downturn: Chelsea were relegated in 1988 after losing a play-off final with First Division Middlesbrough. Losing 2-0 from the first leg, Pat Nevin weaved into the box and crossed for Gordon Durie to finish, but Chelsea were unable to find a breakthrough for the second goal. Nevin had a glorious chance late on but shot tamely into the goalkeeper's arms. The match again was marred by crowd trouble as Chelsea fans invaded the pitch thanks to an open security gate. It took police 30 minutes to restore order.

Record Breakers

Dark clouds had gathered over Stamford Bridge after relegation. Pat Nevin was sold to Everton, what's more, the terraces at Stamford Bridge were closed by the FA for the first six matches of the season after the trouble against Boro. But Campbell remained focused and bought tough-tackling Graham Roberts from Glasgow Rangers to boss the back four, and Peter Nicholas from Aberdeen to shore up the midfield with his determination and tough tackling. Campbell also brought in Ian Porterfield as his assistant, a calm and collected man who perfectly balanced fiery Bobby. A 2-1 defeat to Blackburn on the opening day didn't bode well, but the goals flowed thanks to a rejuvenated Kerry Dixon, and Chelsea were promoted with a record 99 points, 17 more than second place Manchester City. Chelsea won 29 games that season, a record only matched by the 2005 Premiership winning squad.

LEFT: Kerry Dixon celebrates his hat-trick against Barnsley in April 1989.

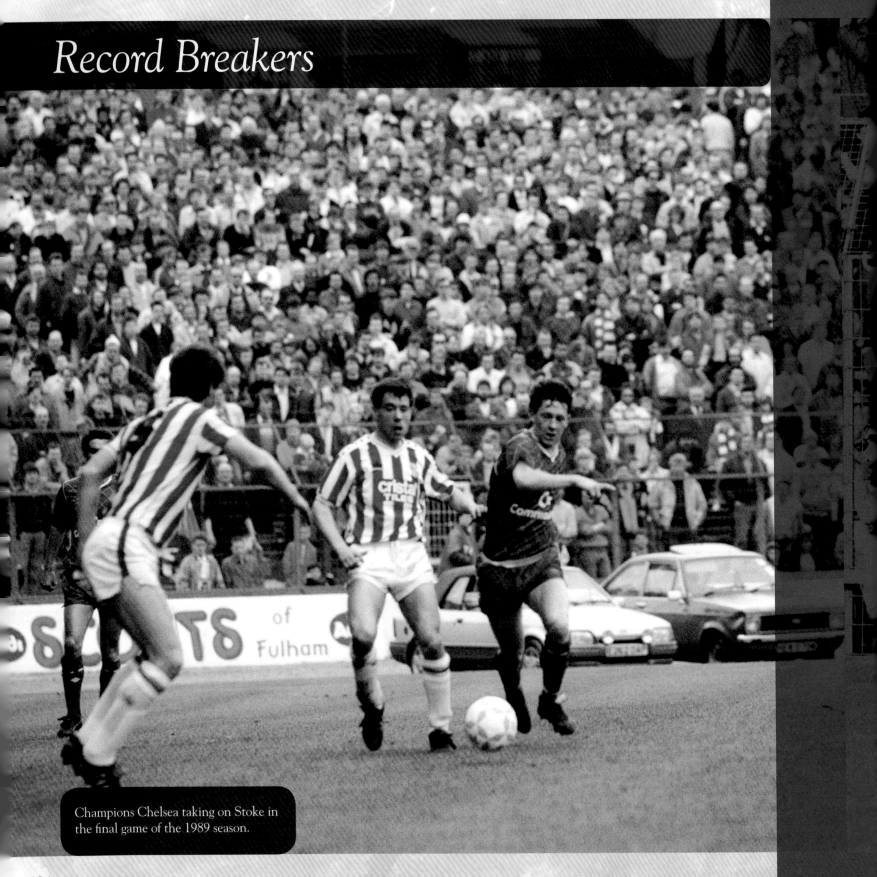

Record Breakers

Champions Chelsea taking on Stoke in the final game of the 1989 season.

The party is on as Chelsea beat Leeds 1-0 on 22nd April 1989, with one fan in an ambulance getting the best view in the house.

Dave Beasant and Tony Dorigo lead the celebrations.

Peter Nicholas dribbles round some motors.

–LEGENDS–

Gordon Durie

Signed from Hibs in 1986, Gordon "Jukebox" Durie was a tenacious striker instrumental in the 1989 promotion campaign. Kerry Dixon in particular seemed to flourish while playing next to the Scotsman, scoring 25 league goals in the promotion year, although Durie himself was the top scorer when the club was relegated a year earlier, with 20 goals. Groin injuries restricted him to only 19 appearances and five goals on the club's return to the top flight. Durie left at the end of the 1991 season, claiming he needed to move north because his wife was homesick. He did move north, but didn't make it as far as Scotland – he joined Spurs.

Durie celebrates a goal with Dennis Wise.

FOOTBALL –STATS–

Gordon Durie

Name: Gordon Scott Durie

Born: Paisley, Scotland, 1965

Position: Centre-forward

Playing Career: 1981–2001

Chelsea Career: 1986–1991

Club Appearances: 153

Goals: 63

Scotland Appearances: 43

Goals: 7

Not even blood could stop Durie giving his all for the cause, even if it was sometimes in vain, as it was during Chelsea's play-off defeat in May 1988.

Campbell's Super

Bobby was originally appointed John Hollins' assistant in 1987. Until then, he'd had a rather uneventful managerial career at Fulham and Portsmouth, where he won promotion from Division Three. Campbell took over as caretaker manager when Hollins was sacked. After winning promotion in 1989, Chelsea finished fifth in the top flight in their first season back and

finished 11th the next season. In 1991 he was moved "upstairs" by Ken Bates and named the chairman's personal assistant. He was replaced by his own assistant manager, Ian Porterfield.

LEFT: Bobby Campbell hugs Graham Roberts after promotion in April 1989.
BELOW: The gaffer pours a brew for John Bumstead and Kevin Wilson.

The ZDS Cup

The 1990 Full Members Cup squad celebrate their victory over Middlesbrough. Renamed the Zenith Data Systems Challenge Cup (or ZDS), Chelsea won 1-0 thanks to a Tony Dorigo goal in front of 76,369 fans. Skipper Peter Nicholas, who'd taken over from Graham Roberts, was only the second Blues skipper to lift a trophy at Wembley. He was also named man of the match.

Graham Roberts celebrates scoring on 12th November 1989 against Sunderland.

Graham Roberts

Often remembered more for his FA Cup and UEFA Cup medals with Spurs and league titles with Rangers in Scotland, Graham Roberts also left his mark on Chelsea during his two years at the club. He scored 22 goals (13 of them penalties in one season) and was a rock in defence as Chelsea roared back to the First Division with those 99 points. He left for West Brom in 1990.

Midfield Generals

Two of football's most well-known midfielders in the 1990s joined in the same summer. Wise joined for a club record £1.6 million from Wimbledon, while Townsend joined for £1.2 million from Norwich City. Wise was named skipper and won six trophies during his time at The Bridge. Townsend's career as a Blue was shorter – he played for three years before joining Aston Villa. Wise grew into his role more the next season, mainly because he was playing alongside one of his mates, another former Wimbledon midfielder.

FOOTBALL
–STATS–
Dennis Wise

Name: Dennis Frank Wise

Born: Kensington, 1966

Position: Central midfielder

Playing Career: 1985–2006

Chelsea Career: 1990–2001

Club Appearances: 445

Goals: 76

England Appearances: 21

Goals: 1

Bobby Campbell welcomes Dennis Wise and Andy Townsend to The Bridge.

unicorn
The Big Name in Darts

FOOTBALL
-STATS-

Andy Townsend

Name: Andrew David Townsend

Born: Maidstone, 1963

Position: Central midfielder

Playing Career: 1980–2000

Chelsea Career: 1990–1993

Club Appearances: 138

Goals: 19

Republic Of Ireland Appearances: 70

Goals: 7

Honey, I shrunk Dennis Wise.

Vinnie Jones

Jones certainly had an impact on Wise's performances during his two seasons at the club. He joined from Sheffield United and brought with him the confrontational, underdog philosophy he and Wise had shared at Wimbledon. One time at Anfield before a game against Liverpool, Jones and Wise got hold of a black marker pen and wrote "We're Bothered" on the famous "This Is Anfield" sign. To rub salt in the wound, both players scored in the match. It was Chelsea's first win at Anfield in 56 years. Jones left in 1992 to go back to Wimbledon for six years, and after a brief jaunt at QPR he retired. He is now a Hollywood actor and recently starred in *Celebrity Big Brother*.

Jones and manager Ian Porterfield.

John Bumstead

John Bumstead's Chelsea career came to an end in 1991 after 13 years at The Bridge. He went out on a high, keeping the likes of David Platt and Paul Gascoigne quiet in his last matches. A tough-tackling, always dependable midfielder, he spent his final two seasons at Charlton before retiring. "We were such a good, professional side and it was the most enjoyable time I had as a midfielder with Nigel Spackman as a partner," says John. 'We had a really good understanding and John Neal was the best manager I had at Chelsea."

FOOTBALL -STATS-

John Bumstead

Name: John Bumstead

Born: Rotherhithe, 1958

Position: Central midfielder

Playing Career: 1978-1993

Chelsea Career: 1978–1991

Club Appearances: 409

Goals: 44

John Bumstead is congratulated after scoring at Highbury in March 1990.

The Chelsea Pensioners

No history of Chelsea Football Club would be complete without mentioning the Chelsea Pensioners. The Pensioners are residents at the Royal Hospital Chelsea, a retirement home for former members of the British Army. The club was even nicknamed The Pensioners until Ted Drake changed the name in the 1950s. Despite that, The Pensioners have always been welcome at Stamford Bridge and still attend games to this day.

A Chelsea Pensioner manages to get his hands on the FA Cup during the 1970 parade after victory against Leeds.

The Pensioners show off their skills in January 1970.

With thanks to Paul Moreton, Richard Havers, David Scripps, *Loaded* magazine and my missus, Asha, for her patience and now extensive knowledge of Chelsea FC.